Praise for *Reflections of a Purple Zebra*

In *Reflections of a Purple Zebra*, Nancy Wright Beasley is a modern voice struggling in our own familiar territory with the ancient dichotomies of life and death, love and hate, sickness and health, good and evil, joy and sorrow. Nancy never blinks in the struggle, even when the pain is seemingly unbearable, and she never leaves any doubt that the side of love and life will win out. What Churchill called "the black dog" of depression may have its day, but Nancy's joyous purple zebra of life will be the ultimate victor.

Her insights are startlingly original: cradling a dying eagle on the side of the interstate allows her in a strangely beautiful way to understand and even experience her husband's early death. The instinctive hugs she gives and receives in an Indiana church a few days after September 11, 2001, reverberate all the way back to Virginia. Her writer's block evaporates when she meets a 5-year-old on a beach who maps out his plan to become a scientist in the Congo.

Beautifully written, Nancy's stories are about the comfort of family and friends, courage in the face of death and evil, wisdom, the connectedness of all human beings and ultimately the joy of living. I commend them to you.

—Randy Fitzgerald chairs the English and Mass Communications Department at Virginia Union University. He was a longtime public relations director at the University of Richmond and columnist for the *Richmond Times-Dispatch*.

Reflections of a Purple Zebra

ALSO BY NANCY WRIGHT BEASLEY

Izzy's Fire: Finding Humanity in the Holocaust

Reflections of a Purple Zebra

Essays of a Different Stripe

NANCY WRIGHT BEASLEY

Tandem, a division of Palari Publishing
Richmond, Virginia

All events depicted in these columns are based on true
events. The characters are authentic.

Library of Congress Cataloging-in-Publication
Data
Beasley, Nancy Wright, 1945-
    Reflections of a Purple Zebra : essays of a
    different stripe / Nancy Wright Beasley.
       p. cm.
    Collected columns.
    ISBN-13: 978-1-928662-90-7
    ISBN-10: 1-928662-90-0
    1. Title

PN4874.B3632 A25
814′.6 — dc22

        2006030977

Manufactured in the USA on acid-free paper

        www.nancywrightbeasley.com

        Edited by Carla Davis
        Illustrated by Sarah Matthews
        Book design by Garie Ann Hutson

        First Edition
        10 9 8 7 6 5 4 3 2 1

For my beloved late parents,
Posie Harless and Beulah Mae Wright;
my brother, Harless Wright; and
my sisters, Janet Watkins and Doris Wright.

They should all be rewarded, especially after having
seen their names in my column on multiple occasions
and then graciously agreeing to let me continue living.

Acknowledgements

How does a zebra count her stripes? Well, I'm not sure, especially since she can't possibly see them all at one time. That's how I felt as I tried to decide which folks to thank. There has been a multitude of supporters, especially Susan Winiecki, Carla Davis, Chad Anderson and Karla Novick and many other staff members at *Richmond Magazine*.

The "Z" project has been cooking for a long time and has literally been pieced together from halfway around the United States. Carla Davis did an admiral job of editing the work after she relocated to Utah. Sally Huband, Inge Horowitz and Diane Dillard of Richmond, Va., offered vigilant encouragement on the home front. Sarah Matthews, also of Richmond, contributed illustrations that added zest to the work. Garie Ann Hutson spent countless hours graphically nudging and tweaking the columns from Indiana, piecing the puzzle together until it became a book. Thanks to each one of them and to Robert Johnston for always giving valuable computer support.

I'm also fortunate enough to have many wonderful friends and colleagues in Virginia Press Women, the Society of Professional Journalists, the School of Mass Communications at Virginia Commonwealth University and the Brandermill Rotary Club. Members of these organizations have stood by waiting to offer assistance, whether professional advice or just a much-needed hug. You are all very special folks.

So many others have encouraged me that it

would be impossible to name them all, but I would be remiss not to thank Neil November and Howard Kellman for their special support and seemingly endless belief in my work.

A very special thank you as well to those individuals who opened their hearts and allowed me to write about them and to the unseen and unknown individuals who have read my columns and found them enjoyable. That is all a writer could hope for.

— Nancy Wright Beasley

Table of Contents

Table of Contents

Foreword

My introduction to Nancy Wright Beasley was through an impromptu visit to my glass-front Main Street office in Clarksville, Va. She stuck her head into the news bureau of the *Richmond Times-Dispatch*, introduced herself, welcomed me to my new job and offered her support from nearby South Hill, only 30 minutes away down U.S. 58. I was on deadline and couldn't talk long, but the inflection in her voice was that of a kindred spirit, a friend whom you knew you could count on. Nancy knew well the job I was taking on. She was legendary in Southside Virginia for her gripping coverage of the Mecklenburg Correctional Center's death row escape in 1984 for my then-competitor, *The Richmond News Leader*.

After that initial visit in December 1990, life and death intervened. Nancy lost her husband, Oscar in 1991, moved from South Hill to Fredericksburg and then returned to Richmond to care for her aging parents. I've worked with Nancy professionally since 1996, when I became the editor of *Richmond Magazine*. She can cover hard news with the best of them and then turn around and write a personal essay that will bring you to tears.

Since April 1998, she has written a monthly column for *Richmond Magazine* that twice has won the silver award for personal column writing in the national City and Regional Magazine Association Awards, overseen by the University of Missouri's Department of Journalism. In that competition, she's in the company of writers from *Texas*

Monthly, Los Angeles Magazine and *Yankee Magazine,* among many others. Of her work, the judges wrote, "Nancy Wright Beasley's columns are intensely personal. Whether she's writing about the Columbine massacre or the Holocaust, she lets readers inside her life to see not only what she thinks, but why."

Over the years, these columns have put her in touch with many old friends. Often the e-mail to me starts out, "I would like to get in touch with Nancy and maybe talk over old times," as Hannah Cornelius wrote in July, 2006, after Nancy did a column about an Iraq War veteran. Others she reconnected with include her childhood friend and former next-door neighbor Diane Dillard. Still others were readers who became friends. Carolyn Charnock, a resident of Tangier Island, Va., had received a column Nancy wrote about losing her husband shortly after she lost hers. She kept that column and tracked Nancy down in Richmond. The two met on the island, another column was born, and she and Nancy still keep in touch.

The name of Nancy's column started out as "A View From the Top," part of an expression used in a card sent to her by her sister after Oscar's death: "When the going seems all uphill, just think of the view from the top." In her very first column for the magazine, Nancy wrote that she would be examining life and how some folks have lived it and how they have gotten strong in the broken places.

And, as the CRMA judges wrote, she doesn't exclude her own life. She opens that up wide, too, examining the ugly, the beautiful, the serious, the silly and the sad that have occurred along the way.

She's had the chance to relive events through her column: the marriages of both of her sons, the birth of two grandchildren, caring for her elderly parents until their deaths, and goals met, such as pursuing a second master's degree in children's literature.

All these columns have come with many "discussions" between Nancy and her two editors at the magazine, myself and Chad Anderson. What to leave in, what to leave out, what to cover next, what to skip. And we have made mistakes on both ends.

My biggest was not fully explaining a magazine redesign to Nancy and the need to shorten her column title to one word, so that it would fit in with the new look and typography of the magazine. When she saw it in print the first time, she was so distraught, she couldn't speak with me. I had forgotten the genesis of her original title, and the timing of the column's name change coincided with the anniversary of her husband's death. I felt like a heel, and, in turn, Nancy said she may have been overly attached to those five words.

Nancy let us run with the name "Reflections" and has continued to hold a mirror up to her own life as well as those of her family, her friends and the many strangers she encounters who turn into friends.

In Nancy's monthly mirror, we all can see a bit of ourselves. And she never fails to explain to us why.

—Susan Winiecki
editor of *Richmond Magazine*

*But they that wait upon the Lord shall renew their strength;
they shall mount up with wings as eagles; they shall run,
and not be weary; and they shall walk, and not faint.*

Isaiah 40:31

1

New Point on the Horizon
Steering toward the rest of my life

THIS COLUMN WAS BORN because my two sisters love me. Of the many gifts my oldest sister, Janet, has given me, the most priceless one was when she spoke at my husband's memorial service in 1991. Oscar and I shared 28 years together and had two beautiful sons before he died at the age of 49.

At his service, Janet read a poem from *Out of Africa*. The movie, based on a true story, was written about another young man who, like my husband, was greatly loved and died too young.

Janet later sent me a consoling letter trying to help me overcome the grief. The letter described the man in the movie who, before his death, gave his compass to the woman he loved with the instruction to "pick a spot on the horizon each day and steer by it." Janet said I must look for that spot on the horizon, set my compass for it and follow it — no matter how shaky I might be.

My compass has been out of whack since my husband died. The horizon hasn't been clear, nor many points on it. The best of guiding instruments wouldn't have helped.

After his death, I could not have survived without the support of my family — especially my sisters. During the times of deepest depression, I tried to remember that God never shuts a door that he doesn't open a window. When the door was shut on my husband's life, I believe my sisters opened every window they could find to help bring the sunshine back for me.

During that time, I received a special card from my other sister, Doris. That isn't unusual. She has a sense of timing that comes from staying close to her family.

The card has a mountain scene with a rainbow in the distance over a group of pine trees. Superimposed over the tops of the trees is the verse, "When the going seems all uphill, just think of the view from the top."

After reading the card several times, it became apparent to me that something sent just to brighten my day would serve as an inspiration for the rest of my life. Instinctively, I knew that I had found the point on the horizon to steer by, that I would frame the card for my desk and that the verse would become the title for the column I've always wanted to write.

I have a passion for writing. I believe it was stamped on me at birth. If I had been asked, I probably would have chosen another profession, because this one hurts sometimes. No, it hurts a lot of times. That's what happens when you look deep inside people and write about their "heart" times.

Doris also has insight about that. She says, "There's no growth without pain. Sometimes it's not a joy ride, but you wouldn't trade it because you surely wouldn't want to always stay the same."

Her words remind me of one of Hemingway's sentences in *A Farewell to Arms*. He wrote, "The world breaks everyone; then some become strong at the broken places."

That's what this column will be about. It will be about life and how some folks have lived it and how they have gotten strong in the broken places. I'll address various subjects like veterans and the homeless. I'll focus on everyday life and, at times, will address the special circumstances that senior citizens encounter.

I've always been in awe of older people. Besides babies, I think they may be the only ones who deserve to be called "real" people. In my opinion, the rest of us are just "practice" people.

Some of these older folks may be willing to share their secrets of survival with you and me. Along the way, I'll be looking for two other women who reached out and helped pull their little sister through the hardest time in her life. If that happens, I hope they'll allow me to write about their view from the top. ≋

April 1998

2

Blue Mornings
What I learned from a rooster and a galvanized bucket

P EOPLE WHO LIVE IN the city miss a lot, especially blue mornings and the lessons that farm animals can teach. There's nothing quite like getting out of bed and standing on the porch before the sun comes up.

While the rooster is doing his best to alert the world that a new day has dawned, the cows mill around at the barn making a wailing, mournful sound, calling out to the hands that will feed them and relieve the pressure of their milk.

Sometimes the sky is a muddled purplish blue with streaks of white. Pretty soon, pale pink shows up followed by a little orange, and suddenly the sun bursts open on a new day.

I used to stand barefoot on the front porch looking at the dawn just before going out to milk my cow, Buttermilk. Recalling those times brings back memories of growing up on a farm in Christiansburg, Va. That's where I learned to love the feel of mud between my toes and to enjoy the sheer abandon of jumping from a high tree while hanging on to a grapevine. I can still feel the rush in the pit of my stomach that comes while daring to leap from tree limb to tree limb without falling. I've envied birds their ability to fly ever since catapulting through the woods in late afternoons.

My brother and two sisters and I all had responsibilities. I can't remember much about theirs, but I sure recall mine. Because I was the "baby girl," as my Daddy called me, I got off rather light when it came to chores. Besides milking my cow, my other job was to rob the hens.

Mama always gave me a galvanized bucket to gather the eggs in. She never failed to caution me about being careful not to drop it. That bucket was almost as big as I was. It took both my hands to hold it above the ground when it was filled with eggs.

Each day, I'd pick up the bucket, being careful not to squeak the handle. I'd sneak up on the chicken pen and stand just outside the fence, waiting for that blamed white rooster to go around to the back. If he saw me, he'd chase me all the way to the henhouse. Of course, when I emerged with the eggs, he would be standing at the door waiting to chase me again.

Day after day, the quest went on. I'd try to get to the henhouse and he'd try to catch me. I don't know why he didn't follow me into the henhouse, but he never did. He probably instinctively knew there was only one way out. And I knew he was there waiting for me.

At the time, I was sure he was as big as I was. When that rooster fluffed his feathers, he looked 5 feet tall. I think he took delight in tormenting me. I was probably the only human he had ever seen who was short enough for him to conquer. Every day when I'd pick up the bucket and head out to gather the eggs, my heart started thumping so hard I could taste the sound.

One day I made it to the henhouse without the rooster seeing me, found the eggs and was on the way out when he came upon me by surprise. He laid back and tried to flog me. His spurs were several inches long and sharp enough to rip holes in my legs.

I was convinced I was going to die. He ran circles around me while I stood frozen in one spot. I was too far from the house for anyone to hear my squalls of terror. I kept the bucket between me and the rooster. He was getting madder and madder because he couldn't reach me.

I knew it was a do-or-die situation. When the rooster backed up to catch his breath, I wound up that bucket like a slingshot and took aim. I probably had visions of David and Goliath at the time or I wouldn't have had the nerve to try to overcome him.

With all my might, I slung that bucket and it found its mark. I recovered the bucket and, spilling eggs as I went, ran wildly through the gate. Shutting the gate, I turned to see the rooster wobbling toward the henhouse. I was halfway hoping he'd die and knowing I'd be in trouble if he did.

I have told no one of my experience until this day. The rooster lived, but he learned a lot of respect for that bucket. After that, he hightailed it to the other side of the pen when I even got close to the gate. Some days, I'd squeak the handle just to watch him run.

Like many other experiences on the farm, that lesson taught me a lot about life. I learned that I could experience my worst fear and still survive. And it taught me how to dig in my heels and stand my ground when the winds of life blew hard enough to almost tear my clothes off.

I seldom see a blue morning or hear a rooster crow that I don't wonder if there is some child trying to conquer a daily chore and inadvertently learning how to face the world. ≋

June 1998

3

A Daughter's Dance
How do you thank a mother for all she's done?

I'VE ALWAYS LOVED TO dance. Even as a child, I can remember picking up the edges of my dress and twirling around when I heard music. I would even hold my kittens and pretend they were my dancing partners.

One of my favorite Christmas presents was a little orange-and-white record player. It only played 45 rpm records, but I thought it was the finest gift any teenager could receive.

My love for dancing grew as I did. When I dance now, I can't help but think of my mother and how grateful I am to her that I can dance, or even walk.

I contracted polio when I was 7 and in the second grade, before the Salk vaccine was discovered. I remember being very sick and being taken to a doctor with a red mustache. I remember my father carrying me in his arms to a waiting car and being whisked off to the closest major hospital, 40 miles away from our farm in Christiansburg, Va.

My mother told me recently that my father had been too upset to drive. My Uncle Fred and Aunt Edith, knowing they were exposing themselves to a contagious and deadly disease, volunteered to take us. After a spinal tap, I was admitted. I was too sick to protest being left alone in a foreign world.

An epidemic of polio was sweeping the country. Children and adults were dying daily; scores of others were being crippled for life.

I was placed in an isolation ward in sterile surroundings. Nurses had to wear a special robe and mask every time they came into my room, disrobe in an adjoining room and incinerate the outer clothing they took off.

I didn't feel as alone after my mother sent me a frog that I named "Squeaky." When I pushed his belly or feet, he made an awful noise that made me laugh. I also received a little pink handkerchief with ducks around the border that my Aunt Christine sent in a get-well card.

When I had to get an injection, which was often, I bit down on Squeaky's foot. He hollered, I cried, and the little hanky got wet. It's been more than 40 years, and the teeth marks are still on the frog's brown boot. The tearstains have long disappeared, but I still have the tiny handkerchief.

I was in the hospital for weeks in an isolation ward. For visitation, the nurses would take me out on a sun porch where my parents and I could see each other through a glass partition. We could talk by phone, but I wasn't allowed to touch them. I remember feeling the warmth of my mother's hand when she put it up to the window so that

I could match my hand to hers.

By the grace of God and those hands, I survived without any paralysis. I was bedridden for about six months after I was dismissed from the hospital. During that time, I watched a daily ritual. My mother would go to the springhouse to get water every morning and every afternoon. She would lug those heavy buckets uphill; sometimes she had two in each hand. Inside the kitchen, she would lift the water and pour it into a big round galvanized tub that was waiting on a hot wood stove.

As the steam started rising, she repeatedly filled the bucket, lifted it from the stove and poured the almost-scalding water into an oblong tub on the floor. She would carry me to the water. Then the screams would begin. She had to fight me to stay in the tub while exercising my legs. I remember my father, tears running down his face, often pleading with her to stop. She ignored his pleas by saying, "She's going to dance again."

She went through this backbreaking ritual when she wasn't chopping wood, milking cows, churning butter, cooking or sewing for my brother, my two sisters, my father or my grandfather. In her spare time, she helped me with my lessons. I missed half a year of school, but I passed with flying colors.

Some of the best memories I have of that time revolve around the afternoons when she would read Bible stories to me so that I would take a nap. Sometimes, she fell asleep beside me. Little wonder.

I have often looked back on those days and

tried to think of a way to repay her. I left home when I was 17 to attend college. I married the next year and have lived away from home for more than 30 years.

My husband died almost seven years ago — the same month we began our 28th year together. My internal compass got out of whack after that, and I wandered around aimlessly without a lot of purpose for a while. Two years later, when my mother was diagnosed with breast cancer, I found the right direction.

My mother is 78 and has emphysema, making oxygen a necessity 24 hours a day for the past four years. When I learned of the cancer, I knew that the time had come for me to use my hands for her. I relocated to Richmond, Va., just six-tenths of a mile from where my parents have lived for about 40 years. Tom Wolfe says you can't go home again, but I've come close. I can get to my parents' house in five minutes, three if I run the light.

Working as a freelance writer gives me the chance to walk out of my office at any time. I have the unlicensed joy of being able to take roses to my mother that I grew in my yard, run errands for her, help prepare meals and make cakes for my Daddy or just listen as they reminisce about the old days. I can't believe I am so fortunate.

At times, I'm terribly sad about my mother's health. I can't imagine my life without her, and I don't want to try. But one thing's for certain: I'll always be grateful that God allowed me to live long enough to have this opportunity.

When I run up the back steps to my parents' home, sometimes I think about those months when I was sick and couldn't walk. My Daddy tells the story about finding Mama milking one day during the time I was sick. In her distress, she was sitting on the milk bucket and milking onto the stool. He tells it to be funny, but then I see just a hint of tears in his eyes and remember how he looked when Mama was giving me her version of physical therapy.

Sometimes now Mama points to me and tells people, "She's the mother and I'm the child." I try hard not to encroach where she can still do things. I see her struggle and it rips my heart out. I understand how she must have felt when I was sick and sometimes wobbly on my feet.

This is a hard place to be, just like when I had polio. But we'll manage and we'll do the best we can because where one is weak, the other is strong.

We've always been a close family. Growing up on a farm teaches you about interdependence. You learn that your family members are the most important people on earth. Thank God, my father and two sisters are always close by. Between the four of us, and occasionally my brother and his wife, who live in North Carolina, we'll pull through this together.

I wouldn't have it any other way. ≋

July 1998

4

The Path to Education

A longer route can be more fulfilling than a straight shot

V ISITING A PERIODONTIST
is not my idea of fun.
It doesn't make sense that
I would pay someone to
hurt me. While I appreci-
ate Dr. Stephen Saroff and
his gentle chairside manner, I don't enjoy all
aspects of my visits to him.

There has been one notable exception. That day
remains in my memory because Wendi Tudor, Dr.
Saroff's office assistant, reached out and changed
my life.

On my way to the office, I had planned to stop
and have a scholarship application photocopied.
Class registration at Virginia Commonwealth
University was just six weeks away, and I had
depleted earlier scholarships. But I forgot to make
the copies, so I carried my papers inside and asked
Wendi if she would do it for me.

"Sure, be glad to," Wendi said, in her usual exu-
berant way. She went to the copier and I went to the
chair.

As I was leaving, Wendi asked, "What happens

if you don't get this scholarship?"

"Well, I don't know," I answered. "I made this bargain with God some time back. I told him if he would provide the money, I would go to graduate school. I've held up my end of the bargain so far, but right now he seems to be slacking off."

"I hope you don't mind," Wendi said, "but I made an extra copy. My mother needs to see this." I stopped myself just short of reminding her that as a writer I could probably provide more interesting copy if her mother really needed something to read. Wendi explained, "My mother belongs to an organization that provides grants and scholarships specifically to assist women who, for one reason or another, have had their education interrupted."

For once, I was overqualifed for something.

I entered Chowan Junior College in 1963 when I was 17. The following year, I ended up marrying the third boy I dated on campus.

Fourteen years and two sons later, my husband encouraged me to enroll at Southside Virginia Community College, which was near our home in South Hill.

It was 1978. I fell in love with school all over again. As the highest honors graduate in my field of study, I spoke at my graduation ceremony. I had the pleasure of publicly thanking my family for eating so many pot pies, and I got to pay tribute to my parents. My father is illiterate and my mother only has a sixth-grade education, but they are some of the most educated people I know. They lit a fire in me that burns to this day when it comes to education.

I subsequently enrolled and graduated from

Virginia State University with a bachelor's degree in individualized studies. By that time, colleges had started allowing credit for experiential learning to be applied toward an undergraduate degree.

Three years earlier, I had been hired as a state correspondent for *The Richmond News Leader*. Although my editor, Jon Donnelly, knew that I had no writing experience and had never been published, he took a chance on me.

When I started classes at VSU, Donnelly and Jay Strafford, another *News Leader* editor, went to bat for me by saying that I had either met or surpassed the requirements for numerous journalism and editing classes. Consequently, I was given 18 hours of credit, plus six more hours of credit from a sales position I held.

I graduated from Virginia State in 1981. By that time, my husband had re-entered college as well, going on to obtain his undergraduate degree at age 42. For seven years running, he and I were in school, either individually or collectively, along with our two children.

Unfortunately, my husband began having severe complications from diabetes. Through the next 10 years, Oscar lived in a literal hell of continuous medical procedures that included, but were not limited to, thousands of laser shots in both eyes, cataract surgery, peritoneal and hemodialysis and a kidney and a pancreas transplant. On Sept. 23, 1991, 20 days after his 49th birthday, my husband went to his eternal reward.

The following year, I moved to Fredericksburg to take a new job that included educational benefits. By 1994, I had completed three courses in a graduate program at Mary Washington College when my mother was diagnosed with breast cancer. She was already on oxygen 24 hours a day due to emphysema.

Contrary to what Tom Wolfe says, you *can* go home again. After 32 years of absence, I moved to a house six-tenths of a mile from my parents' home. People often ask me, "Does your mother live with you?" to which I answer, "If she did, she wouldn't be living."

Wolfe was right, at least in part, because there are so many changes that come about in the trials of life. It is sometimes hard to meld our personality differences, but we manage well with a mixture of love and laughter.

I have always had ties to Richmond. One friend, George Crutchfield, former director of the VCU School of Mass Communications, tried unsuccessfully for at least 15 years to get me to enroll in the graduate program. When I moved here and scholarship money was provided by the Virginia Press Women and the National Federation of Press Women, I enrolled. Now that I've asked him to chair my thesis committee, George is probably sorry he finally succeeded.

I choose to attend school and work on a part-time basis because I want to be available to help my parents. While trying to survive as a freelance writer, I have learned that the world will not only let artists starve, it will let writers starve as well. I guess that is what you call equal opportunity employment.

I'm finally beginning to see some light at the end of the tunnel. I now write on a regular basis for several publications, and I am negotiating to write a nonfiction book. In April, I became a columnist for this magazine, and in May I became editor of *FiftyPlus*, a monthly publication geared to folks over the age of 50. Once again, I found myself overqualified for something.

Although I'm facing this fall semester without scholarship funds, I'm really not afraid. Somehow I know that it will work out. I didn't know how my education would be paid for when Wendi introduced me to her mother, Ginger Mohlie, and an incomparable contingency of women. The P.E.O. Sisterhood has not only provided me with school funds, they have called and encouraged me. They have sent me cards and Christmas presents. Through them, I have witnessed the personification of the saying, "It is more blessed to give than receive."

There is a Scripture that reads, "To whom much is given, much is required." I can assure you that I do not take scholarships lightly. Because others have believed in me, I have dared to believe in myself and in my work.

As you might imagine, I am a very determined person. I believe that each of us has a preordained role to play in this life, but many of us never find out what that role is. How blessed I am that I've had help in discovering mine.

By the way, I never got word back on the VCU scholarship application Wendi photocopied for me, but I do approach my periodontal visits with an altogether different attitude now. ≋

August 1998

5

On Eagle's Wings
A resolution of death

WHAT WAS A BALD EAGLE doing in the middle of the interstate? As I watched, he spread his wings and tried valiantly to escape the oncoming traffic. One car passed without making contact, but the downdraft of the wind caught the majestic bird and plummeted him into the path of a second car.

The driver didn't attempt to slow down as his car hit the bird throwing it to the side of the road just in front of me. Thinking that I was seeing an apparition, I pulled over as quickly as I dared and ran to the wounded bird. I believed he was real only after touching his back and caressing his smooth feathers.

It never occurred to me to be afraid. I was overcome with remorse that such a magnificent creature was losing his life and would never soar again. I stroked his back for a moment before taking him into my arms. As I cradled him, he did not resist or try to pull away. I rocked him gently feeling the warmth of his body next to mine. I told him how beautiful he was and that he wasn't going to die alone.

I will never forget his eyes. Before I touched him, he pierced me with the wild and fierce look that all eagles possess. I paused for a moment remembering times when I had shuddered after looking at the glaring eyes of an eagle from a distance. But, this day, I had no reservations.

As I watched, a transformation took place. When I touched him, a calmness came over both of us. I knew that he was dying, and he knew that he was dying. By some miracle, I was being allowed to hold this beautiful, wild creature the last seconds he would spend on this earth. I could not help but cry as his life slipped away.

As he looked up at me, his icy eyes mellowed and became gentle. The vibrant yellow color turned almost translucent and reminded me of the pale color of newly sprouted corn silk. I saw an acceptance in them — a knowledge that his life was leaving his body and that someone was there to hold him as it slipped away.

As I knelt by the interstate with hundreds of cars whizzing by, I was reminded of the Scripture that says even a sparrow doesn't fall without God noticing. I knew that I, and no one else, was supposed to be there at that rare and precious moment.

Somehow, I believe I gave that eagle something special. I feel almost certain that he was never touched by human hands. He had no bands on his legs. I estimated that he was less than 5 years old because he still had a few mottled feathers that only young eagles have.

By allowing me to hold him and share his last breaths, the eagle also gave me a priceless gift. Without knowing it, he gave me an experience that I missed when my husband died.

I loved my husband beyond words. We met in college and spent 28 years together and shared two beautiful sons. Although he had been hospitalized numerous times with chronic illnesses during our life together, I always managed to be with him most of the time. That changed the night he died.

No words can explain how I feel about leaving him at the hospital. He wanted me to go home and be with my parents. He was not supposed to be in danger and looked better than usual when I left.

Later, I wanted to return to the hospital and be with him. When I told my mother this, she encouraged me to honor my husband's wishes — to stay at my parents' home and try to rest.

When the call came that he was gone, I was inconsolable. As time passes, I realize that he would have preferred that I be with my parents so that they could love and comfort me. I realize now that God had mercy on me. Still, I felt an ache that just wouldn't go away — a nagging remorse that somehow I had let my husband down.

One of my best friends tried to console me about not being with my husband when he died. My friend told me of watching many men die during the Vietnam War and explained that as death approached, it was sometimes embraced with a calm acceptance and resolution. He said that for some of his fellow soldiers, no struggle occurred.

I tried so hard to accept that fact. I wanted to believe that when my love died he simply stepped into a brighter more beautiful place where there is no sickness or pain. I had wondered how he felt. Was he afraid? Or, was there a brilliant light that beckoned him beyond our world? Did he reach out for me and the boys or did he wave goodbye and quietly slip into the spirit world to embrace a love so all encompassing that we can't fathom it?

I never understood my friend's explanation of death until I experienced the eagle's last moments when he, like a fallen soldier, seemed to almost welcome the release of death. It was so quiet and peaceful that it was indistinguishable from life except that his eyes closed.

I want to believe that death was that gentle for my husband. I want to believe that his last breath was peaceful and that somehow he was cradled in someone's arms and was gently rocked until he simply closed his eyes. I want to believe that he experienced what we had talked about so many times—that death would be a time of rejoicing.

My experience with the eagle is a comfort to me. It has transformed my husband's memory into the personification of my favorite Scripture from Isaiah 40 that reads, "...They that wait upon the Lord shall renew their strength; they shall mount up with wings as eagles; they shall run and not be weary; and they shall walk and not faint."

Oscar L. Beasley died Sept. 23, 1991, just 20 days after his 49th birthday. My encounter with the eagle occurred on Jan. 31, 1993. This column is dedicated to my husband's memory and in celebration of the seventh year of his eternal reward. ≋

September 1998

6

Deep Roots

As the twig is bent, so grows the tree

THERE IS A WALL BETWEEN MY NEIGHBOR AND HER world. It's impossible for her to penetrate the wall, but she's doing her damnedest to go around it.

I met her about a year ago when I was taking a morning walk. From the distance, I watched her stilted steps as she maneuvered down her long driveway to the mailbox. With ever so much care, she placed a three-pronged cane on the ground between loose gravel, checking the stability before stepping forward.

A tiny redhead, she was less than 5 feet tall. No bigger than a fifth-grader, she didn't weigh 100 pounds. A brace from heel to knee enclosed her pencil-thin right leg. Her right arm hung by her side.

I sped up my pace, snatched her newspaper from the chute and asked, "Looking for this?" "Yes," she said with a broad smile. "Thank you." Not sure how to handle the meeting, I just hurried up the driveway, gave her the paper and mumbled something idiotic like, "Isn't this a nice day for a walk?" Again, she just said, "Yes."

Since she didn't offer any further communication, I wasn't sure if she could speak in sentences. Making an excuse about being in a hurry, I quickly retreated and walked my two miles with her on my mind. I wondered who she was, if she had family and how she managed with her turtle pace in a rabbit world.

After that, I started leaning her newspaper at her back door when I went walking. A car, which never seemed to move, was always parked next to a handicapped ramp.

Following an out-of-town trip several months ago, I was again out walking, and it dawned on me that I had forgotten about delivering her paper. I almost ran, hoping I wasn't too late for that day. There she was again, carefully making her way to the road. I made up my mind to meet her properly this time.

"Hi, my name is Nancy. What's yours?" With a grin she said, "I don't know." She laughed out loud when I said, "Well, if you don't know, how am I ever going to find out." Again she said, "I don't know." We both belly laughed.

Hoping not to embarrass her, I began to ask questions. Much to my surprise, she was delighted. With hand motions, she invited me into her spacious home.

I learned her nickname is B.J. Not only does she live alone, she maintains her bedroom on the second level, scrubs her own kitchen floor in between her one luxury, monthly housekeeping services, and drives herself to grocery stores, medical appointments or to visit family, if it's a short distance.

Over time, I have met my neighbor's two sons, daughter and Jimmy Harris, one of her brothers, who comes on a regular basis to help with the house and yard maintenance. All of her children and a second brother live a good ways from Richmond, two of the children in other states.

Recently, B.J. suffered a stress fracture in her right leg and is confined to a wheelchair, which she operates with one hand. While she has some drop-by friends and neighbors, her only constant companion is a 10-pound terrier named "Frau" and a set of 3x5 cards with written words on them. She uses the cards, including one with her own name written on it, whenever she can't verbally express what she needs. She wrote the cards with her left hand, after she lost the use of her right arm.

More flash cards, containing her children's names, addresses and ages, are held up for visitors to see and matched to photos that adorn her home.

With an ear-to-ear grin and obvious tenderness, she shows off an infant's photo mounted prominently on her refrigerator. Her first grandchild, Katherine, was born in June. She's looking forward to holding her grandbaby, even though she won't be able to talk to her.

My friend can say more without uttering a word than anybody I've ever met. She has developed a variety of communication forms, including head and hand gestures combined with a few limited words to express herself. She uses an address book, a calendar, even the newspaper to help explain her thoughts.

Sometimes she gets so frustrated she grimaces, grabs her head and just makes sounds for a minute, but she never gives up. With her blue-green eyes flashing determination, she will get her point across, one way or another.

By pointing to an afghan with Lunenburg County scenes on it, she conveyed that she was a native of Southside Virginia. When I asked about her early life, she indicated that her mother was a third-grade school teacher and that her father was a pharmacist, explaining the latter by banging a prescription bottle on the kitchen counter.

When asked about her childhood, she leaned over the arm of the wheelchair, dropped her good hand almost to the floor and moved it back and forth seemingly skimming the surface of the floor.

When I didn't understand, she grabbed the newspaper, turned to the obituary page and said, "This." Her father had died when she was only 5 and she, as the oldest child, learned about responsibility by helping care for her twin brothers.

As best I can learn, the stroke that now limits her life occurred when she was 47, 10 years ago. A divorcée who lived alone at the time, she supervised five employees and managed a large Richmond firm that provides information and support for Virginia's educational system.

She had just come home from work during a snowstorm and parked her car in its usual spot. From that point, she has no memory of that day. A neighbor discovered her lying in the snow beside her car when he came home.

After hospitalization and therapy, her mother stayed with her for a short while, but my friend wouldn't allow dependence on anyone longer than a few weeks. It is obvious that her mother was an inspiration and an outstanding role model.

My friend says that her mother worked and cared for her children alone until they were teenagers. She eventually remarried but was widowed a second time before her death about three years ago.

If it's true that acorns don't fall very far from the tree, then Southside Virginia must be fertile soil for giant oaks whose deep roots give them stability during the most violent storms. ≈

October 1998

7

The Joy of Parenting
Sons who reach out to help

HAVE YOU EVER WONDERED about your effectiveness as a parent?

Don't you wish for an exact how-to manual you could buy that would guarantee success? I've always been amazed that a license is necessary to own a dog, but no one's permission is needed to give birth or raise a child.

As parents, most of us blunder along by instinct. For the most part, we do a decent job. Like every other challenge we face in life, we do some things better than others.

Before my husband died, we often talked about whether we had given our sons too much and whether it would cause them to be selfish. When the two of them squabbled, we wondered if they would ever learn the beauty of the Golden Rule.

When I was living in Fredericksburg a few years back, something happened that would have pleased my husband and assured him that we had succeeded, at least in one way, as parents.

Two weeks before Christmas, my older son, Oscar Jr. ("Beau"), had a party at his home in Alexandria. As I entered the house, I saw a giant vase sitting on the bar that separates the kitchen from the living room. The vase was empty. I made an offhand remark about the jar being for a nonexistent piano player and asked if my son needed money. He shushed me into silence by saying, "Later."

When the house was overflowing with guests, Beau stepped up to the vase, clinked it with a knife, and asked for everyone's attention. He announced that he had set the jar out for guests who chose to contribute. He told of some kids in his church whose father was incarcerated. They were facing a bleak Christmas.

The vase changed all that. Needless to say, I had to leave the room for a few minutes.

My younger son, Jason, was due in from college the next week. His brother and I planned to surprise him by taking him out to dinner.

He was late. The phone rang. I answered it hoping he was OK. The conversation went something like this:

"Mom, this is Jason. Now don't get excited. I'm OK. I'm at the King's Dominion exit, and I'll be home in just a few minutes."

Jason wanted to know if he could bring home a stranger for Christmas. He had picked him up on the highway near Myrtle Beach, SC, and had spent the past seven hours driving him toward Washington, D.C., the hitchhiker's destination.

He continued, "It's not what you think, Mom. Hal is really a nice guy. Yes, I know you've told me a million times not to pick up hitchhikers, but Hal is different. Yes, I left the keys in the truck. I wanted to keep the heater going for Hal. It's cold out here. Yes, I can see the truck. Yes, I have my money in my jacket. Mom, will you relax? I tell you Hal is an OK guy."

I agreed to feed Hal but told Jason that he couldn't stay with us through the holidays. I tried to reason with him: Not only did we not know Hal, but also I was a widow who lived alone.

I had to call for reinforcements. With his brother on another phone, Jason repeated the story. When Beau also objected to keeping the man, Jason quietly asked, "How can the two of you call yourselves Christians? You're always saying that we need to think of other people. Well, I am thinking of somebody else. It's Christmas, and it's cold. I really like Hal, and I don't want to leave him alone."

After a moment, wisdom prevailed. We agreed that Jason would take Hal to a restaurant and wait for us. I didn't know how it was going to happen, but I promised him that we wouldn't leave his new friend stranded.

I called the Salvation Army. Got an answering machine. Tried to call some churches. No answer. Finally I remembered Charlie Hill, a man who had been Jason's youth minister when we lived in South Hill, Va. Charlie was currently employed by Falmouth Baptist Church in Stafford. I breathed a sigh of relief when he gave me the name of the Thurman Brisben Homeless Shelter. I held my breath and called. There was room at the inn.

Beau and I quickly put together a Christmas

stocking of sorts. While he got the cookies and the candy canes, I rummaged through my grocery cabinets for small cans of fruit and other packaged goods and stuck them into a Christmas tote sack decorated with poinsettias. Finally, Beau pulled out his wallet and stuck some money into the bag.

We met Hal, and, true to Jason's word, he was different from any hitchhiker I had ever seen. He was immaculate. And articulate. He stood up to meet us, offering his hand. He used the proper eating utensils, ate slowly and lightly, laying his knife across his plate after cutting his meat. He was so bright that I had to stretch my mind to keep up with his vocabulary. That's why Jason had liked him so much.

He was very knowledgeable about marine science, Jason's major in college. Hal said he used to be a college professor on the West Coast but had worked his way around the country over the past several years and was on his way to see his son. We talked for two hours. During that time, Jason was obviously pleased that he had brought us together.

After dinner, we took him to the homeless shelter and gave him the makeshift Christmas stocking. He was grateful for a place to stay and seemed genuinely touched with our small gifts.

Standing outside the shelter, I asked his last name. Upon hearing it, I questioned if it was Norwegian. Hal expressed surprise that I recognized the origin. Jason laughed and said, "My mother's mind has taken her places she'll never go in person."

At that moment, huddled in a cold parking lot with a stranger, I realized that both of my sons had reached deep inside their hearts and given to people they didn't know and likely would never see again.

With those acts, they had also taken me places that I had never gone before. I am satisfied that I will visit those places again. ≋

December 1998

8

Unforgettable Faces
Juvenile judges make life-altering decisions

For Bonnie C. Davis, 1993 was marked by a major career move.

After serving a decade in the legal world, three years with a private law firm and seven as a prosecutor in the Chesterfield County Commonwealth's Attorney's Office, she was appointed as the first female judge in Chesterfield County's Juvenile and Domestic Relations Court.

It was her second career switch. In 1977, she entered law school after teaching eighth- and ninth-grade English for six years.

You can say she's always been a soft touch for kids. When not cloaked in her barrister's robe, Davis draws an exaggerated smile from ear to ear; dons a red, yellow and blue outfit, huge tennis shoes, a curly red wig and a hat complete with a giant daisy; and visits children and elderly folks in hospitals and nursing homes. To develop her clowning skills, she attended a six-week course at John Tyler Community College.

"I wanted to do something that would be a service to children other than what I do professionally," she says. But there were fears for this clown. "I thought that seeing sick children would upset me. It does have an effect on me, but I get the biggest boost when I see those faces."

It's the memories of children's faces, in hospitals or courtrooms, and often in especially repugnant cases, that stick with Davis. And, even though she sees a jaded view of the world from her side of the bench, it doesn't discourage her.

"If I didn't believe that I could make a difference, I couldn't do this work. I truly believe that it is a gift to be able to deal with it on a daily basis," she says.

"When I get discouraged—and you do in this environment—I always read this." She picks up a scrap of paper from a case she had prosecuted that has laid on her office credenza for years. "It's from a 10-year-old girl who was dragged from her home by her mother's boyfriend and raped in the woods behind her house.

"When the man was being led to the lockup, the double doors to the courtroom were opened and the child was told the outcome. She came over, hugged me said, 'Thank you.' I'll never forget that. She held out her little hand and gave me a piece of paper."

The note, written on a scrap of paper lent to the child by a social worker, reads, "I just wanted to tell you, you're great at your job!"

"That kind of thing makes the difficulties worthwhile, whether it's a team effort or me personally," Davis says.

"While I was the one who was in court present-ing the case," Davis explains, "I played a very small part in the total effort. The real work had been done before we got into that courtroom. I truly could not have done it without the support of [many] other professionals [who work with juve-niles].

"I often wonder about that little girl. I believe that her psyche will be damaged forever. I don't think that anyone ever gets over that horror, not even an adult woman."

Davis shares court responsibilities with fellow judges Frederick G. Rockwell III, Jerry Hendrick Jr. and current chief judge Harold W. Burgess Jr., each of whom hears about 5,000 cases per year. While they realize that every case cannot be successful, all of them are particularly proud of the record that Chesterfield County holds regarding juvenile offenses.

"This county has a 'zero' tolerance where juve-nile crime is concerned," Burgess explains. "For three or four years, we have had less than two dozen DUI cases involving juveniles between the ages of 16 and 18. That's phenomenal when you realize that we give out about 400 licenses in this county each month." Any child found guilty of possession of alcohol or an illegal drug substance in the county forfeits his operator's license for a prescribed time.

Unfortunately, there is an increase in other cases in the court, which influenced the decision to build a new courts building, scheduled to be com-pleted by the end of 2000. The new complex will provide space for the current judges but can be expanded to accommodate six or more courtrooms. The 12th Judicial District also encompasses the City of Colonial Heights, which requires one of the four judges to hear cases there for one-and-a-half days each week.

The majority of Chesterfield County cases involving adolescents are crimes against property, larceny and breaking and entering, Burgess says. "We do have young people commit violent acts, but not near the number that cities have."

Burgess admits that it is difficult to incarcerate a child. However, there are rewards. "Some parents are very angry when a child is sentenced, but many have come back to me and said, 'Thank you. Now I have my child back.'"

Burgess and Davis both say that custody cases can be heart wrenching.

"We probably hear more custody cases than any other kind," Burgess says. "They can be particularly tough, especially when you have two good parents who are equally able to offer the child a stable environment.

"However difficult the circumstances may be, we just have to believe that our work makes a difference, whether it involves a juvenile or a whole family."

Davis nods in agreement and says, "While some cases will affect you for a lifetime, you just have to keep your personal feelings in check and make the best decision you can." ≋

April 1999

9

In a Fix

For Daddy, anything can become good as new

MY FATHER'S TWO-CAR garage, basement and outdoor building all look like a gigantic yard sale after a hurricane has hit.

Bits and pieces in the storage spaces range from antiquated farm implements to a tool bench weighed down with the worst collection of leftover, bent or otherwise abused tools that you can imagine. But, everybody knows that beauty is in the eye of the beholder.

My father's "treasury" has been carefully cultivated over the 44 years that my parents have lived in Richmond. Anyone within hearing distance has been aptly warned about moving anything or even trying to bring order to the chaos. It's okay to borrow, but you'd better make darn sure he sees you bringing it back.

When my mother threatened to leave home if a path wasn't cut through the basement, my older son and I volunteered for clean-out duty with the wild idea that Daddy might be willing to part with a few things.

Mama sat in a chair giving either an affirmative or negative nod to each object my son and I held aloft. Many of the things she had previously sent to the trash pile had miraculously reappeared because Daddy had squirreled them away in the corners of the basement.

While we ripped and tore, Daddy paced between the basement door and the ever-filling pickup truck like a displaced Mama cat with a kitten in her mouth, running to and fro trying to find a new home for her baby.

Because Daddy had to inspect each object before parting with it, the effort ate up three-fourths of a day and ended up as a mixed blessing. The space was clean, but I came down with a horrific allergic reaction to the mold in the dank basement.

My father probably thought it poetic justice that I had been stricken for disturbing his domain. I'm still being blamed when anything is missing.

A lot "takes a missin'" at my parents' home, primarily things my father has laid down and completely forgotten. He owns at least six grease guns because he can never find one when he needs it.

When he can't discover what he's looking for, Daddy harangues for days, claiming how someone has snuck into his basement and hauled off one of his possessions. It has never occurred to him how much courage it takes just to walk into the basement, much less pick up anything.

Over the years, we have learned to just track down the utensil ourselves or stop up our ears until the current blue streak is over. Sometimes he sheepishly admits that he has discovered the lost object exactly where he left it, but that's the exception rather than the rule.

Often, the tools are rusted and inoperable from having been left in the open for several months. They get relegated to the tool bench, waiting for him to "find a day to oil 'em and make 'em good as new" again. My father is 85, and I haven't known him to find a day yet, so the pile just keeps growing.

Although my father appears miserly, he has actually brought home an enormous amount of worthwhile objects over the years that other people have discarded simply because they are tired of them or because it's easier to replace rather than repair them.

My parents were born in the early 1900s, before electricity had snaked its way through the mountains of Virginia. They have lived through tough times and see no need to waste anything.

The Depression added to their outlook. Neither has forgotten what it was like to do without basic necessities. They have never put much stock in "new" things and have always "made do" with what they had, especially Daddy.

I was telling my mother recently that I needed a wheelbarrow and was on the way to buy one. My father appeared from out of nowhere, threw up his calloused hand like a stop sign and said, "No need to do that. I got one out in the pickup truck that I just found. All it needs is a new tire. I can fix it myself."

Knowing his words had sealed my fate, I

agreed to locate the tire and hope for the best. Several trips to lawn centers and many phone calls later, I told my father that I had given up the hunt and planned to buy a new wheelbarrow. Thoroughly disgusted with me, he said, "Just don't you worry yourself 'bout it. I'll find that tire myself."

Darned if he didn't. It took him two weeks and God knows how many miles, but he bought a new tire for $13 and proudly told me that he'd also repair that "little bitty" hole in the front end of the wheelbarrow. "It will be good as new with a few brads and a scrap piece of metal," he said.

I accepted the wheelbarrow, declining the patch job and marveled at my father's ingenuity. He had saved me money, resurrected a broken wheelbarrow and had given us both a new lease on life.

It made me realize that my father could teach us all a lesson about recycling. If New York City were populated with more men like my father, not as many of the Big Apple's discarded cores would be making their way to Virginia's landfills. ≋

May 1999

10

Writing a Life

Greg Donovan's two favorite subjects are
poetry and his students

IF CLICHÉS WEREN'T ANATHEMA
to poetry, one would
be tempted to label
Gregory Donovan as the
absent-minded professor.
Donovan, who teaches a
variety of literature classes
at Virginia Commonwealth University, forgets
appointments because he doesn't remember to
check his calendar. He dawdles away time playing
the mandolin instead of writing a poetry book he
took a sabbatical to complete. He's willing to sell
his current poetry book to acquaintances for less
than what it cost to publish it. And, he owes his
publisher, the University of Missouri Press, a $1.50
instead of the reverse.

"I didn't write the book to make money,"
Donovan explains with an easy laugh. "I just want
people to read poetry and learn from it."

Donovan, now 48, has learned a lot over the
years. He learned that he was born in Arkansas and
that his birth mother didn't want to meet him. He
learned that he could find solace in books, even

though his adoptive mother punished him for doing so. He learned that he had a deeply spiritual side. He learned that he was a political activist and conscientious objector. And, he learned that he couldn't impart teaching in the same way he had been taught.

He gleaned wisdom while completing a master of arts degree at the University of Utah where he first began teaching in a graduate assistant program. As a doctoral candidate at State University of New York at Binghamton, he was inspired to write fiction by John Gardner, a professor and accomplished writer.

Donovan, who published his first poem in 1972, says that he "lost heart" in writing fiction after Gardner was killed in a motorcycle accident. "I didn't have the courage after that," Donovan says.

"I actually prefer poetry, although it is the hardest work, is the least rewarded and is the most independent."

Donovan, a bachelor, came to VCU in 1983 and gained tenure in 1991. He worked as an instructor, a visiting assistant professor and director of the creative writing department for eight years, a responsibility he still shares on a rotating basis with other creative writing faculty.

Donovan describes himself as "an irascible, independent working-class intellectual." He took a turn at a blue collar job after obtaining his undergraduate degree in 1972.

"I had gotten disgusted with the hypocrisy of my teachers and I didn't want anything to do with the establishment," Donovan says.

Instead, he followed a wanderlust. Along with

a college buddy, Donovan spent five years painting houses in North Carolina. He still wears the working-man aura, augmenting it with brown plaid shirts and tee shirts that match his deep azure eyes. He would look just fine hanging out of a bucket truck in a lumberjack commercial.

Donovan has recently been hanging out at his Oregon Hill home and only has a few months left to iron out the wrinkles in his brain before returning to the classroom. Although time is fleeting, he claims that he's still in a "rest and recharge" warp instead of actually admitting that he is successfully producing poetry—a disclaimer he uses so as not to jinx the productivity of his work. While he is working very diligently to meet his fall deadline, Donovan gladly carves out time to talk about his favorite subjects—his students and poetry.

"Teaching is a sacred responsibility and I don't take it for granted," Donovan says. "I find myself delighted by the imagination and freshness of the inventions that my students try. Some of them have accidental moments of brilliance but then there are the real moments of insight. Oftentimes, they don't recognize their [own] strengths."

Donovan says that he gains strength from music as well as the personal wrestling matches it takes to breathe life into his own poetry. He cites modern day poets Norman Dubie and Philip Levine as being two of his favorites, while referring to British romantics Keats and Coleridge as "touch-stone" poets from whom he's learned so much.

Learning is the epitome of living for Donovan. Conveying that wisdom to his students is a privilege he looks forward to every time he steps into a classroom.

"None of my poetry students have gone on and become well known yet, but poetry is a long germination to any sort of success.

"Poetry won't make you much money, but you end up taking a kind of perverse pride in doing this thing that most people can't do. Most people are actually afraid of it, but they will read it because there is no other way that human beings have for organizing experience that supplants language."

Donovan believes that writing sometimes offers us a chance to lead a better life. "Sometimes the way we achieve that better life is not by actually getting good advice but it is experiencing things that are astonishing or beautiful or amazing and writing about that."

As a child, Donovan used to hide in the bathroom in order to read because his adoptive mother did not appreciate books. Now he says, "Reading was my life." Donovan is "a real proponent of imagination" and strongly encourages his students in their exercise of imagination as readers and as writers.

"The more they can do that, the more they'll have fun having been alive. So often people think of poetry just as being a narration that comes out of the poet's life.

"Poet's are good people who feel deeply about things that all of us feel. They just express themselves better than others do.

"But, that's not all of what poetry is. Some poets have the same imaginative large canvas that any novelist might have. They make you see things in a new way that you would never have thought of before.

"Norman Dubie has a poem about Queen Elizabeth that is worth all the films that have come out about her. 'Elizabeth's War with the Christmas Bear' is profound, revealing and heartbreaking."

Donovan admits that there is some heartbreak in writing poetry. "Let's face it. Most poets don't get rich. You can actually make money in writing fiction, but I will write poetry regardless of whether one person or 1,000 people read it.

"I want to believe that a person can pick up my work and feel a deep sense of delight, but it doesn't have a lot to do with me. The work should have a life of its own." ≋

June 1999

11

A Wayward Mind
Directional dyslexia scrambles the brain's road map

MY HUSBAND OFTEN JOKED that if he really wanted to get rid of me, he'd just take me two blocks from home and drop me off. With my sense of direction, he was convinced that I'd never turn up again. He was exaggerating, but only by a little bit. In fact, I'm the only person I know who has ever gotten lost in a Holiday Inn parking lot.

It seems there are a lot of folks like me. So, how come, when we seem to function normally in most areas, we stay lost—even with a map in our hands?

It took me years to figure out that I wasn't "dumb as an oyster," a term my beloved pegged me with early in our marriage because he couldn't understand the severity of my problem. The clincher that convinced him that I wasn't faking happened when we were leaving a restaurant parking lot on Midlothian Turnpike several years ago. My entire family had just shared a meal together and planned to rendezvous at my parents' home about a mile away. I turned onto the road and was driving silently. After about three miles, my husband said, "If you're going to your Mama's, you'd better turn around."

While familiar places were sometimes hard for me to find, going to a new area often turned into a traumatic trip to never-never land. I can't even retrace a path that I just followed a few hours earlier, unless I have the directions written in reverse order. While I've burned up a lot of gas over the years, I've also met some interesting people and seen a lot of beautiful country homes. One experience in particular comes to mind.

I was working for an electric cooperative in Mecklenburg County at the time and had an appointment to interview a farmer who lived near the Virginia border. After several miles and several futile turns, I stopped at a country store and called the office for directions. I was mortifed when the dispatcher radioed one of the linemen and said, "Beasley's at a pig farm in North Carolina. Can you go rescue her?"

This problem has not always been funny. As a small child, I instinctively learned to enter school through the same entrance and count the doors in the hallway to make sure I was stepping into the right classroom. After I got lost in the hall one day delivering a note for the teacher, I never volunteered for that duty again. Too frightening.

High school was worse. I had to change classes, which were on different floors, and plow through a maze of 1,300 students. Because we were organized alphabetically by our last names, I learned to follow my classmates whose names ended with a "W."

College proved even more daunting, but the third boy I dated on campus had a sense of direction like Sacajawea. That may be the reason I married him. Finally, I felt safe. Now I could get there from here.

Over the years, I have learned to overcome some of my fear of traveling to new places, but I was at least 50 before I realized that I had a learning disability. I accepted the condition, with relief, and understood for the frst time that I had no control over it.

Inge Horowitz, a Richmond teacher who specializes in learning disabilities, has helped me more than anyone to understand what is happening, or rather, what is not happening in my head.

"You are a right-handed person which means that you are 'left-brain' dominant," she said recently, explaining that we humans are wired backward.

"While there is input from the right side, language is basically housed in the left brain." She explained that the right brain controls spatial properties. Based on that, I figure my right brain must be empty.

Recently I have begun using the words "directionally dyslexic" to describe my situation to others. Inge explained that spatial problems like mine are very specific and while nonverbal learning disabilities may be a part of dyslexia, that condition usually centers primarily on problems with reading, writing and language skills.

The Learning Disability Council of Richmond addresses such problems. Inge recently coordinated the publication of the 1999-2000 edition of the

Learning Disabilities Directory, a free publication that is available through the council, in local libraries and in parent resource centers in all Virginia school divisions.

The directory, which touches every area of daily life, is only one service provided by the Council, which was founded in 1973 to address issues affecting children and adults with learning disabilities.

Their only source of income is a parent guide and workbook, *Understanding Learning Disabilities*, which costs $19.95. It can be ordered through the Council. Inge also introduced me to a magazine named *Their World*, a publication produced by the National Center for Learning Disabilities. The magazine lets me know that I'm not alone in my disability and there are many, many others with much more severe problems than I have or could even imagine. ≋

July 1999

12

Behind Young Eyes
Children can be the best teachers of how adults should raise them

W HEN MY OLDER SON WAS ENTERING school, I encouraged him to "be big and responsible" and painted word pictures about the "fun" he'd have. Like any 6-year-old, he was thrilled with new shoes and a Spiderman lunchbox but less excited about leaving home. I assured him that he'd meet new friends and that the bus driver knew where we lived.

He was prepared for the first day. I wasn't. When his chin started quivering and he wrapped himself around my legs like a grapevine, I fought for composure while coaxing him to "just stay today."

We finally agreed to separate. Evidently he adjusted quickly, but it was one of the longest days of my life. Seeing him roll off that yellow bus was a thrill, even if his new jeans were torn, all his notebook paper had been given away and his thermos had an unmistakable jiggle of broken glass. Nothing mattered except the reaffirmation I felt from his gap-toothed grin and immediate request for Pop Tarts and milk.

All seemed right in the world — until dark. After reading him a bedtime story, I slipped into bed beside my husband. We shared a special moment about how "manly" our little boy had become.

I was almost asleep when I felt my son's presence. He didn't say a word. Just stood there beside the bed until I opened my eyes and asked him what was wrong. I was so thankful for the darkness when he finally whispered, "Mama, is motherf — er a bad word?"

I could barely breathe. In less than 24 hours, my son's life had been inextricably changed. He now belonged to the world.

I carried him back to bed and caressed his cheek, trying to brush away the dirt that was clinging to him. I explained that he might hear other words that he didn't understand and that we would talk about them if that happened.

I doubt he remembers the incident, but I shall never forget it. I also lost some innocence that night. I hadn't thought about the effect that unfamiliar children would have. I believed he was safe at school. I suddenly realized that no safe haven exists and that his father and I couldn't protect him from people, their attitudes or their actions.

The same sick feeling came over me recently while I was watching the news and eating my dinner. When I saw Colorado's Columbine High School students running for their lives, my food became tasteless. I watched in disbelief, learning of innocent children being murdered by not-so-innocent children. Those scenes were recreated until I wanted to scream, "ENOUGH!"

I wanted to ask the newspeople, "What are you doing to reward the law-abiding, hard-working and loving parents and their children who go to school each day, behave themselves and grow up to benefit society?"

I believe I could introduce the media to several students. The seniors in the Chesterfield County Public Schools were given a writing assignment last fall. They had a variety of subjects to choose from. About 2,600 completed essays, which were sent to professional writers who critiqued the students' work.

After the first 25 essays, I called Lynda Gillispie, the instruction specialist who coordinated the new project for the county. I told her that I was tremendously impressed with the quality of the students' work and agreed to take more essays. I wanted to see if I had just happened upon a high-achieving group in the first batch.

After reading a total of 650 of those essays, I believe I can draw a fair conclusion. Those teenagers, who reflect a good cross section of society, created some of the most poignant work I've ever read. Their optimism gave me a new jolt of hope for our future.

I laughed at some, cried at others. I read about teens who were academic achievers, team captains and school leaders. I read about car wrecks, unwed mothers, depression, drug and alcohol abuse and numerous family troubles, including the deaths of siblings and parents.

While several essays disturbed me, more impressed me. These young adults wrote about how they were the caregivers for terminally ill parents. They described how they helped their siblings with their homework and how some also worked — not one, but two — jobs to help feed their families while attending school themselves.

There were heart-wrenching stories about straying into problems and heart-warming descriptions of how they managed, through various guiding forces, to find the right path again.

More than one student wrote of their admiration for a teacher, a coach, a family member or a parent who believed in them when they didn't have the strength to believe in themselves.

Those essays made me think about the responsibility of being an adult. Isn't it more than just caring for our own children? Could it be that all of us are somewhat accountable for what is now being played out in high schools?

Those essays triggered a quote that I've remembered for more than 25 years. I don't know who wrote it, but the poignant words bring home the accountability that every adult has to help train, educate, encourage and guide the generations that follow.

How different our world might be if we reminded ourselves every day: "Be careful what you do. There may be a child listening. There may be a child watching. There may be a child trying to make up his mind." ≋

August 1999

13

Transplanted
Holocaust survivor still loves America despite U.S. policy in 1930s

SOME NAMES ESCAPE me, but not Henry Moss' name. Moss isn't really his name. It's Moszkowicz. At least, that's what it was when he was liberated from a concentration camp in Poland at the end of World War II. Moss came to America in 1951 with only his name and a bag of clothes. He got to keep the clothes.

"When I came here, they said I couldn't speak English, and I wouldn't be able to learn how to spell it, so my name was shortened to Moss," the diminutive white-haired man says quietly. "I wish now that I had never changed it," he adds while dabbing at his crystal blue eyes.

Moss' sister, her husband and their son also survived the death camps. Every other Moszkowicz family member perished. The sister's family came to America but moved to Israel where she died several years ago.

"My family operated a sweater factory in Europe," Moss explains. "North Carolina needed garment factory workers, so I went. I didn't like it, so I came to Richmond, Va."

Moss managed a variety store on the corner of Grove and Libbie avenues but eventually retired after working as a salesman for American Parts Company, which was owned by Israel Ipson and his son, Jay, also Holocaust survivors. Moss, who is about 80, retired in 1996.

About 33 Holocaust survivors now live in Richmond. Their lives have been documented in the Virginia Survivors' Room, a special room dedicated to survivor artifacts in the Virginia Holocaust Museum, which was established in Richmond just over two years ago. Like Moss, many of the survivors either shortened or changed their names to assimilate to America's lifestyle.

I didn't know about his name-change at first. That came out as he haltingly shared a small bit of his history. He recounts chilling scenes of carnage that he can't forget and explains that he has never married because he has constant nightmares. But, mostly he talks about his life after coming to America.

When he uses the words "United States" in a sentence, he pauses and says, "God Bless America," then finishes his sentence. No matter how many times he refers to the United States, he follows it with "God Bless America." It's like hearing a bugle call in mid-sentence, the jolting transition drawing attention to the phrase.

Another time, this idiosyncrasy might not have stood out so much. But as I heard him, I couldn't help but wonder if I could do the same after an event like the Holocaust, especially given my newfound knowledge.

While researching the World War II era, I learned some things about my country that I didn't want to know. I learned that the United States refused to allow a ship to disembark about 900 Jews in May 1939, even though most of them were on a waiting list for U.S. admission.

The SS St. Louis, a German ocean liner, carried occupants who believed they had managed to escape Nazi atrocities by purchasing Cuban visas. They planned to live in Cuba, hoping America would eventually accept them. When they arrived, Cuban authorities declared all visas invalid but 30, those for six non-Jews and a few Jews with special visas. The ship's owners ordered its return to Germany.

The ship hovered just off the East Coast, near enough to see the lights of Miami. Appeals of help to the United States were ignored, and the U.S. Coast Guard patrolled the waters to make sure no one jumped to freedom. The Netherlands, Britain, France and Belgium agreed to each take some of the passengers. Nazis and life in concentration camps killed all of the Dutch deportees and all but a few of those left in France and Belgium, while the 288 left in England survived.

I learned that Franklin D. Roosevelt had knowledge for years that genocide was taking place in Europe but turned a deaf ear to pleas from both humanitarian groups and his wife. While the U.S. was more understanding than most countries, Roosevelt, along with many other world leaders, took a laissez faire attitude toward the killings. He authorized U.S. aid when it became apparent that the world would discover his negligence and the fact that top management in the U.S. State Department had been withholding reports of genocide from the public, as well as forestalling visas repeatedly.

I learned that our Congress did not support the Wagner-Rogers bill in 1939 and 1940, opting to let the bill die in committee rather than give asylum to some 20,000 Jewish children, even though various Jewish organizations promised financial support for the children until they could be returned to their families in Europe. Through long-held anti-Semitic prejudice, it was believed that "20,000 children would soon grow into 20,000 ugly adults." England accepted the children, as well as many others throughout the war years, in a program called Kindertransport.

Though I am no history scholar and believe it is nearly impossible for a layperson to discern the intricacies of government and foreign policy, I can't understand why it took so long for the United States to take action against the mass genocide in Europe. Historical records indicate that Roosevelt may have known of Hitler's plans to completely annihilate the Jews as early as 1939. Hitler erased one-third of the world's Jewry between 1933-1945.

What I have learned dispelled my belief about America's part in providing humanitarian aid in WWII. American soldiers certainly sacrificed and, like all the Allied forces, were welcomed as heroes into the pits of Dachau, Buchenwald and Auschwitz, to name a few. Even after the untold agony and sacrificial deaths of a multitude of soldiers — all hoping to bring peace — thousands of

Holocaust victims died in the camps just days after the liberation because the aid had been years in coming.

Of several million deaths attributed to the Nazis, more than 6 million were Jews; 1.5 million of those were children. Among them were Henry Moss' nieces and nephews. So, how can he say, "God Bless America" in such a way that you know all three words are capitalized? He says he can do it because America gave him an opportunity and he will always be grateful.

Henry Moss lost not only his family name, but, save three members, his entire family and all their history, yet he breathes a prayer for America at the mere mention of the country. His words are magnified by the fact that Sept. 1 marks the 60th anniversary of Germany's invasion of Poland, the beginning of World War II. ≋

September 1999

14

Power of the Word

Often the most important journeys are those
of the mind

M Y MAMA HAS A LOT OF
sayings. I think she inherited
most of them from her mother.
Sometimes, even since I've
become an adult, she drudges out
the one I heard most often as a
child: "Two heads are better than
one—even if one is a cabbage
head." There was never any
doubt about which one of us was the cabbage head.

Another one of her favorites is, "You can do
anything you set your mind to." I often wanted to
ask her, "Does that really mean 'anything?'"
Somehow I never had the nerve. Besides, everybody knows that mothers are always right.
Nobody questions a mother but God. Nobody with
any real sense, that is.

Mothers have a built-in thermometer for knowing when things are right or wrong or when you
can accomplish something or not. And, their sheer
belief in you gives you the courage to try harder.

My Mama will be 80 on October 22. She grew
up during the Depression, married at 18, bore four

children in 6.5 years and has remained married to the same cantankerous man for 62 years. She has experienced many disappointments in life, yet she still sticks to the belief that anything is possible. One of her favorite sayings is, "Nothing beats a failure but a try."

Many years ago I set a goal to become a freelance writer by the time I was 50. I remember talking with my mother about the idea. She said, "Well, if anybody can do it, you can." So, I shouldn't have been surprised when I ventured out on my own at age 48 and now, six years later, have passed both the half century mark of my life and attained my goal of becoming an independent wordsmith.

Although I've been writing for more than 20 years, I still find it hard to believe each time I have a column published. For some odd reason, columns are different than writing under a strict deadline. A personal column affords the opportunity to meander a bit and the luxury of turning phrases several ways before choosing the one I like best.

Since I've never taken a journalism class, I haven't the vaguest notion how I became a writer. I think it may have started way back when I was a child growing up on a farm. We lived in Christiansburg, Va., at the foothills of the Blue Ridge Mountains. There was no television and no inside plumbing. I can't remember much entertainment except my beloved Grampa Wright playing the banjo and my Mama reading me books, especially a big red Bible storybook that now graces my library shelf.

My mother always had a love affair with

words. Her idea of family fun was to line up my brother, my two sisters and me and ask us to guess the definition of words she found in this big black book. Little did I know what effect that dictionary would have on my life, or the set of *World Book* encyclopedias my mother bought us children for "casual" reading.

I, too, am fascinated by words and always have been. It never ceases to amaze me that between the covers of a book is a journey waiting to be taken. I never realized how true that was until my younger son commented to an acquaintance, "My Mama's mind has taken her places she'll never go."

Most of the journeys I've taken have been through books, or more specifically, words.

I attribute my appetite for words to my mother, who recently confided in me that she had once wanted to be an author. She even taught me how to read before I started school. I can still close my eyes and hear her reading, "Run, Spot, run..."

My mother can now read all she wants to, sometimes devouring several books in one week. The reading escalated five years ago in July right after my family got the dreaded news that my mother had breast cancer. Suddenly, she didn't have much energy any more, and she spent a great deal of time lost between the covers of a book.

Along with her energy, the cancer has usurped 75 pounds, but my Mama never complains. In fact, she says it is one of the best times of her life.

We were remarking about the passage of the five-year mark in her plight with breast cancer recently. Over the last several months, I had talked often with her as I followed my friends Julie

Grimes and Mark Fagerburg through Julie's several surgeries for breast removal and reconstruction. Julie was just under 40 when she was diagnosed with breast cancer. I was writing her story when I asked my Mama for advice, since she was an older survivor of breast cancer. I asked her if she had any wisdom to impart.

"Faith," she said, "is the most important thing. I simply couldn't make it without my faith." Turning to the physical side, she said, "The only real effect that cancer has had on me is that I'm so weary." Then she added, "But, I can't even say that's a detriment. Now I can sit down all day and read and people will just say, 'Oh, well, she's sick.' Nobody really expects me to work any more, so I can just relax and read to my heart's content."

Still contemplating my question so as to choose just the right words, she added, "Although I've had to take medication, I've never been in pain. I have my children who are here at my every beck and call, and good friends who help take care of me. I don't really have anything to complain about. When I go to bed each night, I thank God that I've made it through one more day. And, even if I die during the night, I won't have to worry. Then God will take care of me."

Even a cabbage head could not have said it better. ≋

October 1999

15

Toy Story
With needle and thread,
mother makes ends meet during war

Like most little girls, Anne Dalzell loved visiting her grandmother in Church Hill. As a child, Dalzell thought Marguerite Hendrick, whom she called "Momee," was just a typical grandmother who made toys and cooked good meals.

"She was anything but typical," Dalzell said during a recent interview. "I particularly remember two things about her—the way she loved children and the times I went to Broad Street Station to meet the troop trains with her during World War II.

"Momee would actually bring the little neighborhood kids into her house right off the streets to clean them up. Nowadays, she would probably be arrested, but she would take care of anybody's kids, even though she had eight of her own."

Four of those children were sons, all of whom served in the armed forces during the war. That's where the troop trains come in.

"My mother was always worried about my grandmother. Regardless of the weather, Momee would find a ride or take a trolley downtown and stand there handing food and coffee through the train windows to the soldiers. They couldn't get off, but Momee would take messages about calling home for them. I guess she was hoping that someone would do the same for her sons. I was about 8 or 9 at the time, but I still remember the 'Gray Lady' suit that she wore. She did it as long as those trains came through."

Like other women of that era, Hendrick volunteered in a USO canteen and supported the war effort, but she took her dedication a step further. She made dolls and used the profits from selling them to buy bonds in her sons' names.

"I can see her right now using that old peddle Singer sewing machine," her granddaughter recalls. "I don't know what she charged for the babies, but it would have taken a lot of dolls to buy even one bond. I think the least expensive bond was $25, which you had to pay $18 for."

Times were difficult for Hendrick long before the war. Her husband, a traveling insurance salesman, died of pneumonia in 1929, leaving a 40-year-old widow with eight children still at home. She never remarried. Hendrick managed her family by working at a five and dime in Danville, along with assistance from her three eldest children, before moving to Church Hill.

"I'm not sure what gave her the idea for making the babies," Dalzell said. "She originally made them as toys for her grandchildren. Friends began wanting them for their children. Eventually, she also put them in consignment shops, investing in war bonds to aid the effort of her sons, who were serving in Italy, Germany and Guam. Another one served in the states with a medical corps."

Dalzell decided about three years ago to begin constructing similar dolls, dubbing them "Bond Babies." Each one has a tag attached to it, explaining the doll's origin.

"I started just like she did, making them for my grandchildren. Kids today have dolls that do everything, but the Bond Babies are just for hugging. I've been surprised by how adults are interested in them. I think it has a lot to do with the history of Momee's original doll."

Hendrick's dolls didn't wear clothes, but Dalzell's do. She has added another dimension as well.

"I've elaborated on them somewhat. My grandmother's dolls had button eyes," she says. "She made zebra dolls from striped socks and turned red socks into Santas. She made a "Mammy" doll, but I don't think that would be appropriate now, so I make an African doll. And, all of mine also have facial expressions stitched on them."

At Easter and Christmas, Dalzell turns socks into tiny bunnies and angels with wings. None of the dolls, which are all completely washable and safe for any age child, is named, except the generic Sock Monkey, which is constructed from two Rockwood Red Heel Socks. That type of sock has almost disappeared, according to Dalzell, which has probably inspired the web site dedicated to the old-fashioned toy.

While the task is time consuming, Dalzell has no idea how long it takes to make one doll.

"It's like an assembly line, especially when I'm

doing a lot of them," she explains.

The cap, head, body and legs are all one sock, while the arms are sewn on separately. Dalzell sells her dolls to friends, in a North Carolina craft show and at the annual bazaar held in November at the International Mission Board on Monument Avenue. Dalzell retired from the mission board two years ago. She still works there part time, but her favorite time is when she is constructing the Bond Babies.

She reflects on her life, as well as her mother's, and how her grandmother influenced both of them.

"I think my mother and I both inherited some of her strength," she says. "My father died 30 years before my mother. She established an interior design business and did very well, although she never remarried. I divorced young, worked and had primary responsibility for raising five children and also never remarried.

"My grandmother had such spiritual strength. I used to go to Leigh Street Baptist Church with her. I know she must have spent a lot of time praying for her sons. There was fierce fighting overseas, and you didn't get instant information back then. One of my uncles says Momee must have written to each of them nearly every day because he would get bundles of mail in Guam when they caught up with him. She made them feel special, even though they were overseas.

"She was such a rare person. I'd like to think that I can pass along a little bit of her spirit with each Bond Baby." ≋

November 1999

16

Lasting Impressions
Mom's yuletide generosity spans generations

CHRISTMAS IS A TIME OF celebration of faith. Along with that, most of us enter the month of December with an air of expectation and hope that a family squabble won't mar the event, or make it downright impossible. You may also hold dear some special memories or traditions of that holiday, and no matter where you are, they come barreling back to remind you of either an especially good tradition, or a bad time, that you just can't seem to forget.

I was reminded of how similar people's lives are when I was recently reading an unpublished family history written by Hank Cox, brother of Gene Cox, Richmond's long-standing news anchor at WWBT-NBC 12. I discovered that a Cox manuscript was in the making during a conversation with Gene about a year ago. Recently he offered me the privilege of reading a rough draft.

Through 281 pages, brothers Gene, the eldest, Ben and Hank cavort through the skirmishes of teenage tribulation of having a Baptist preacher for a father and a Latin school teacher for a mother. It was a trial for Truett and Meriam Cox to keep their sons on the straight and narrow. As you can imagine, it was not all fun for the parents or the children.

The story describes how the Cox teenagers upheld the notorious rebelliousness of "preacher" kids before becoming upstanding, successful businessmen, good husbands and fathers—sons any parent would be proud of. But, that was a long time coming, and Hank, who has written award-winning fiction, does an admirable job of portraying teenage revelry punctuated with church services whose colorful descriptions left me crying with laughter.

As the book ended, there was a final poignant description of their mother, who although orphaned as a young girl, went on to educate herself and many others along the way. She instilled a love for words that continues to thrive in the hearts of all her sons. Hank describes his mother's last Christmas with her mother, who was dying of diabetes, and how Meriam, unaided by any adult, trudged through snow not only to help her little brother and sister cut down and decorate a tree but prepared a dinner for what would be their last Christmas celebration as a family.

Meriam held the memory in a soft place and chose not to remember the hard parts, like having to chop the wood to thaw frozen milk before preparing the meal. The story made such an impression on Hank that he never forgot it and used it as a fitting tribute to his mother at her memorial service when he was evoking family memories.

I, too, have considered writing a book of my own family's history. If I ever accomplish that, I'll also include a story about my mother and a Christmas some five years ago that I shall never forget.

My mother had learned six months earlier that she had breast cancer. To add insult to injury, she already had emphysema and a ripe aneurysm. Twenty years before that, she had been totally disabled from public work after several heart attacks. No one asked me, but I thought the cancer was a bit much, given the other medical problems my mother was already enduring, which included dragging an oxygen tube around behind her 24 hours a day.

But, my mother, like Meriam Cox, seemed to take her lot in stride. I remember that Christmas because I truly thought it would be my mother's last (but thankfully it wasn't). None of the four children said it, but I think we were all wondering about it privately.

After a sumptuous traditional yuletide dinner, the grandchildren started delivering presents. While the squeals of excitement and flurry of wrapping paper were dying down and packages were being stacked in opposite corners according to family designation, my mother looked at my father with one of those knowing glances that married people often share.

A few minutes later, my father stood slowly and walked outside. That's not unusual. He takes a break sometimes during long family gatherings and can be found sitting quietly on the porch studying the stars or talking to Stub, his snub-tailed cat. No one thought it unusual that Daddy left the noisy den, but we did wonder what he was bringing into the house when he reappeared with a huge black plastic bag slung over his back and a deep grin on his face.

It had been decades since he had played Old Saint Nick, and he was enjoying the suspense we were all feeling. I knew it was going to be extra special because there was a hint of a tear in his eyes.

To our surprise—no—to our amazement, the bag held a personal treasure trove—four hand-made quilts, one for each child. The gift, like the one Hank Cox got from his mother's fragile Christmas, inspired me to write the following:

It was Christmas 1994
All had been fed
The presents bared
Daddy quietly left the room
And reappeared
Like Santa
A bulging sack
Thrown over his shoulder
With a sweet smile
He placed the bag
At Mama's feet
Slowly
With deliberate movement

She pulled the prizes
From the bag
One at a time
Handmade quilts
Nine diamond pattern
Made especially for
Each child
Colors painstakingly chosen
To fit each personality
Daddy cried
And I did, too
The room became small
So much love in a bag
Unleashed all at once
Seemed dangerous
Mama had sewn the quilts
On a treadle sewing machine
While enduring breast cancer
And emphysema
Making oxygen a constant necessity
Who says there are
No more heroes
In our world? 〰

December 1999

17

The Best Day of the Year
Resolutions from 1999 bear letter and love

Oₕ, Lordy, I just checked the calendar. That means I have to face what I resolved to do last year in this space — report to you on how well I have kept my 1999 resolutions.

Among other resolutions, I vowed to write more notes and contact old friends in an effort to restring the thread of understanding that brought us together in the first place. I started by making a list of those folks and kept records of when I wrote to them.

I received some very warm responses, as well as a few surprises. Two letters were returned because the addressees had moved and so much time had lapsed that there was no forwarding address. One note from Isabel Gough, my friend and former co-worker and die-hard writer for *The Richmond News Leader*, was a total shock. I knew that Isabel, who is probably close to 80, decided at about age 70 to purchase and single-handedly run a weekly newspaper in Kilmarnock, Va.

In Isabel's return letter, she lamented the fact that she had to close the paper, not because of her age or failing health, but because she couldn't find suitable employees who were capable of selling advertisements.

Not once did she complain about the numerous things I knew had happened to her over the last decade—that she had been near death and was hospitalized several times for heart ailments and some time had been undergoing dialysis treatments three times a week. This is one regimen that our unfriendly-toward-medical-conditions government considers an immediate and incontestable condition for total disability.

Instead of complaining, Isabel asked me if I knew of any publications that might consider her as a freelance writer. The request took my breath away. My husband, who was 47 when he started dialysis, could barely walk after each dialysis treatment, let alone think about work.

While standing in awe of Isabel's fortitude, I did what any good reporter would do; I called an informed source. Ed Kelleher is an editor whom Isabel and I had shared as state correspondents for the *News Leader*. He is the current assistant editor for the metro section of the *Richmond Times-Dispatch*. Together we came up with some contacts and I sent the information to Isabel. As Ed and I chatted, we marveled at Isabel's "I-can-climb-this-mountain" fortitude and wondered about how many teeth we'd still have or whether we would be walking, much less looking for work, when we became octogenarians. Without a doubt, Isabel will continue to be a source of inspiration for us both.

Another woman I've drawn inspiration from over the last five years was also on my list of folks to re-contact. Again, I was surprised by the outcome. Since I had last seen Barbara Geslock, an accident involving broken bones had left her in a wheelchair for several months. Did she complain? Not a word. Instead, she was grateful that she had just had a home constructed to accommodate her adult son's wheelchair. Now, she said, they could both motivate the hallways without chipping off the paint.

I met Barbara when I lived in Fredericksburg, Va. Our friendship developed as I watched her guide and direct the Women's Resource Center there. I was ending one of my visits at the center one day when I discovered a saying taped on a wall of the bathroom. When I remarked about how beautiful it was, Barbara, in typical style, interrupted her work and retyped it for me.

I keep the words pasted on my computer and read it as a daily guideline to live by. I wish I knew the author so I could give credit, but I don't. Whoever wrote it, though, would be the kind of person (like Barbara) who would be pleased that I passed it on and unconcerned about who got credit for it. I think these few lines have infinite power:

On This Day

Mend a quarrel.
Search out a forgotten friend.
Dismiss suspicion, and replace it with trust.
Write a love letter.
Share some treasure.

Give a soft answer.
Encourage youth.
Manifest your loyalty in a word or deed.
Keep a promise.
Find the time.
Forego a grudge.
Forgive an enemy.
Listen.
Apologize if you were wrong.
Try to understand.
Flout envy.
Examine your demands on others.
Think first of someone else.
Appreciate, be kind, be gentle.
Laugh a little more.
Deserve confidence.
Take up arms against malice.
Decry complacency.
Express your gratitude.
Worship your God.
Gladden the heart of a child.
Take pleasure in the beauty and wonder
  of the earth.
Speak your love.
Speak it again.
Speak it still again.
Speak it still once again.

I hope to incorporate those words into this brand-new century. On New Year's Eve, I plan to sit in my Daddy's straight-backed wooden chair that's sandwiched between an avocado refrigerator and a maple end table that buffers my Mama's easy chair. She and I will count the seconds until the ball drops in Times Square for the fifth year in a row. Daddy will have removed his glasses, dropped them on the dining room table along with his hat and will have commenced snoring in the next room.

I'll be warm, loved and spending time with two of my favorite people. What could be better? Oh, I almost forgot to tell you. I plan to have some of my Mama's famous vegetable soup, made with pork and beans to give it backbone. As I dip soda crackers into the thick concoction, I'll smugly remind myself that I was able to conquer yet another resolution, learning how to make my Mama's soup.

It will give me strength to face the next 100 years. ≋

January 2000

18

The Healing House
Heavy hearts mended therein

ARE THERE TIMES when pebbles of inconvenience turn into boulders in your path blocking anything that remotely resembles peace in your life? When the earth starts to crumble beneath me, I head toward a personal sanctuary I call The Healing House. I know I'm close when I see the sign on I-85 that reads "Meredithville."

The car seems to go on autopilot while I get lost in the dense beauty of the trees. Off Route 1, down a twisted road just beyond a green Dumpster, stands a majestic white house called Oak Shades with stately columns bathed in wildflowers like a Southern belle in multi-layered petticoats. The warmth from an ever-glowing lamp beckons and envelops all who step therein. It's a place of refuge where my vulnerability doesn't matter.

The grand old lady sits on a hill snuggled close-ly by splendiferous oak trees. Several have taken hits from stray lightning and have splintered and fallen, nearly missing the duchess of the estate. She stands opposite a small black mailbox that's perched on two huge slugs cut from a tree trunk and stacked atop each other for a makeshift post. Red brick columns grace each side of the long-driveway that encircles a multi-acre yard. The grass—sometimes mowed, sometimes not—is strewn with all manner of debris left there by four resident dogs whose role in life is to bring any stick, or stray shoe, as a love offering to the caretaker who shares the house with them and a very snooty cat named Sylvia.

I call my friend Gay Neale a caretaker because she is much more than the "lady of the house." She's just as genteel as the 18th-century home, and her arms, like the double doors that welcome visitors from a mammoth porch, are always open. She and the house each seem to beckon a weary soul, "Come, sit down, take a load off, have a cup of tea or a glass of wine."

Once inside, 15-foot floor-to-ceiling windows offer a panoramic view of the garden, the flower beds, the horses in the stable and the cat cavorting on the porch trying to catch hummingbirds as they divebomb a brimming feeder. There is always a grapevine basket in the making laying on the table. Peace reigns supreme.

The house, nor its caretaker, expects formality. They don't care if I wear a pair of jeans and old socks or putz around in a flannel gown all day. Even if I laugh or cry, whisper or shout, or eat chocolate and bagels for breakfast, I'm still loved, accepted and not judged insane. The latter part is especially important.

I met Gay some 20 years ago when we were at an archeological dig at Fort Christanna in Brunswick County. We were both gathering information, I for a newspaper story and she for a book that she was writing on the history of Brunswick County. When my camera jammed, she not only graciously offered to take photographs for me, but would not accept money for the film.

Almost two decades later, she still exudes the same calmness with which she helped pull me from the mire that day. No matter what I dump into her lap, she is able to coddle, nurture and hold it steady until I get my legs again. I've never met another human being quite like her or stayed in a place like her home.

Multiple guests come and go at will, sometimes calling beforehand, sometimes not. They're all equally welcome. At special events held a couple of times each year, the number easily exceeds 100. They drive hundreds of miles to drink in the serenity and retie the bonds of friendship and family. They come laden with food and wine for picnics, with dogs, guitars, canoes and children in tow, to sup and sing, float on the river and spend the night in tents under the oak trees.

Weddings as well as memorial services are held here. Death has visited this house on more than one occasion. I guess that's the beauty of it. The storms of life have come and gone, along with crowds of people traipsing through at any given time, but the duchess remains steady and stands on her original foundation.

The red brick fireplace still splinters the main wall in the living room and offers its backside for picture hanging and herb drying in the spacious kitchen. An aura of solidarity and serenity permeates the plethora of wooden bookcases, the monk cookie jar, the grandfather clock that doesn't work, the roll-top desk complete with a bust of von Goethe and the paintings perched among group photographs of friends and family. At Christmas, a tiny gray porcelain elephant is nestled among the stable animals in the nativity scene. He looks right at home, just like the rest of us who come and camp for comfort.

Even the plants sit close together, either on the two side porches in spring and summer or sprawled up and down the staircases of the three-story house in winter. Camel bells hang on the back door giving a jingle of far-off places when wood is brought in for the sooty black stove that warms the living room and keeps the chill off "the suite" that was added just beyond the kitchen when Gay's mother needed constant care.

Now that her mother has gone to her eternal reward, various writer friends and probably even strangers for all I know use the room, complete with a computer station. In fact, I'm writing this column on it while a bronze Buddha smiles at me from among crystal candlesticks and a crock pencil holder. The caretaker has gone to bed early tonight after bidding her house guest, "Make yourself at home, Hon. You know where the food is. You're welcome to anything here. See you in the morning. Sleep well, my friend."

Burrowing into the bed piled high with blankets, I give thanks for my friend and the strength I have gained from her. I marvel at how she has withstood the storms of life that have nearly torn off her clothes. I often wonder who gave solace to Gay when she was widowed at 32. Where did she get the fortitude to complete her own education, including a graduate degree, while raising and college-educating her children alone? How has she had the strength to help care for, not only her parents and her in-laws, but also her first daughter-in-law, until their deaths and still be standing to give comfort to so many others?

I think I found some of the answers for her deep reserve posted on her refrigerator. Each year, she puts up a new "to do" list. I wrote this while the '98 version was still in place. It starts out with, "Build thee more stately mansions, oh my Soul" and continues in part:

Clean out Snake Room
Clear out catbriar in azaleas
Paint porch furniture
Spray early for p.i.
Drink wine
Get bugs off east wing plants
Join a new organization
Till a garden for Elizabeth
Spin wool
Write a story
Plant grapes, make trellises
Call old friends
And all shall be well
and all shall be well
and all manner of thing shall be well. ≋

March 2000

19

A Cause for Pause

Misdirected prescription prompts health-care examination

I WAS WALKING THROUGH MY LIVING room one day when I saw a stranger looking through the front door windowpane. He caught my eye and held up a white bag. I cautiously opened the door, being careful to leave the storm door closed. I noticed that a truck, clearly marked with a local drugstore's name on it, was parked in my driveway. The gentleman was also wearing a coat bearing the same name.

He asked, "Are you Nancy Beasley?"

"Yes," I said.

"Do you live at this address?"

"Yes."

"I have a prescription for you."

"I haven't ordered a prescription."

"Let me check the address," he said as he turned to look at my mailbox and compare it to the bag in his hand.

"It's right, lady," he said.

"But, you don't understand. I didn't order any medication from your store."

"Well, your name is on this bag and I was told to deliver it."

"Let me see it, please."

Upon examining the bag, sure enough, there was my name and address all spelled correctly along with directions for taking an ulcer medication. I opened the bag to find a prescription for a medication that I didn't need, sent for a problem that I didn't have, from a drugstore I didn't frequent and prescribed by a doctor I had never seen.

This was getting interesting.

I invited the gentleman inside, which, in retrospect I shouldn't have done. He could have been checking out the house so that he could come back later and steal the two overripe bananas I always have in the kitchen. Anyway, he looked so perplexed and apologetic that I opened the door and asked him to wait inside until I called the drugstore.

"Is this the druggist?"

"Yes."

"This is Nancy Beasley. You have just sent a driver to my house to deliver medications that I neither ordered nor take."

"Just send the driver back."

"Just tell me why I got this medicine."

"I'm really busy right now. Just have the driver return the medicine. I'm sorry if you were inconvenienced."

"I'd like to have the phone number of the doctor who prescribed this medication."

"I don't have that available right now."

"I can wait until you look it up on the computer."

"Well, I'm really busy. I'm sorry for the trouble.

I'd really like to speak to the driver."

"I'd really like to speak to the person who prescribed this medication. I've never even been to this doctor."

"It was called in by a nurse."

"From what office?"

"I really don't have time to look all this up right now. I'll call you back later. Just ask the driver to return with the medication."

"The driver and the medication are staying with me unless you give me a phone number of the party responsible for this."

He put me on hold. Another druggist came to the phone. We went through the same ordeal. When he realized that he might have to buy the driver's lunch, he gave me the phone number of the practice where the doctor was affiliated. I returned the medication to the driver, apologized for his inconvenience and thanked him for his patience.

Then, I called the medical practice and asked to speak with the office manager. She confirmed that a) I had never been to their office and b) that no medication had been dispensed to me. She did say that a prescription for the same drug that had been sent to me was called in to the pharmacy I named. A member of the nursing staff had requested it for a patient whose first name was Helen. Neither one of us thought that Helen sounded like Nancy. Helen didn't live anywhere near me. The office manager said she would check out the situation and call me back.

In what felt like seconds, my phone was ringing. Seems she didn't have to wait at all, was allowed to talk with only one pharmacist and wasn't told to "just call back later." She was noticeably upset about the situation and said something like, "I think we may be changing delivery systems in your area." It was just a mistake, you say. Mistakes happen all the time. Yes, they do, but this had been a week of mistakes.

My mother's prescription for Tamoxiphen (for breast cancer) was renewed over the telephone by her physician's nurse. When I went to pick it up, Susanna Dodd, the pharmacist at Ukrop's 60 West Shopping Center, had flagged the prescription. She asked if my Mom had been to the doctor recently.

"Yes, just last week."

"Well, she might want to check with him again. This dosage has been doubled."

Seems the nurse made a mistake when she called it in. The same week, Randy Duvall, another pharmacist at the same Ukrop's, questioned why the dosage of one of my prescriptions had increased when I had been taking the same meds for several years. Two phone calls later revealed that the doctor had made a mistake.

All of these incidents happening in one week was a bit disconcerting.

Don't get me wrong. I'm not bashing nurses or doctors or pharmacists. Many such professionals make my life more comfortable and helped my husband hold on to life through 28 years of chronic illness. Without their dedication, this world would be a sorry place for sick folks.

What I am saying is, "Heads up. Pay attention." These folks are human, too. They get tired and frazzled and become prone to mistakes. In my case, and for some unknown reason, my name came up on the errant pharmacy's computer. Scary, isn't it?

Murphy's Law seemed to be reigning that week. It was a good reminder that it may be best, especially when it comes to medical problems, to "let the buyer beware." ≋

April 2000

20

Food and the Farm
Childhood chores provide cherished memories

TWO THINGS WERE ALWAYS plentiful on the farm where I grew up in Christiansburg, Va. — work and food. They seemed to go hand in hand. When we weren't working, we were eating and when we weren't eating, we sure as heck were working.

I remember learning to milk a cow before I even went to school. When I did get big enough to follow my brother and two sisters down the dirt road to the bus stop, it was always after we had divested the 18 cows of their morning milk. We knew that the same chore awaited us every afternoon, always before suppertime.

Sometimes we got to ride in the open-top Jeep to the bus stop, but only if the foamy milk had been strained through cheesecloth into cast iron cans. Their lids were tapped on tight to prevent spills when we hit a rut in the road. Being little, I didn't understand why the milk was so important. I thought more attention should have been paid to whether the kids fell out the back of the Jeep.

The different forms of milk always fascinated me. One of my fondest memories is of watching the crawdads swim backward in the springhouse around the crocks of milk that we kept for our own use. While the crocks cooled in the streams of rushing water—nature's refrigerator before electricity reached the mountains—an inch-thick rim of cream formed on top. My mother would scoop it off with a long-handled metal ladle and save it to pour over blackberry cobbler.

Other milk Mama poured into churns. One was a huge glass container with a screw-on top like a gallon jar. A paddle was built into the lid. I knew the butter was close to forming when I could see the specks clinging to each other on the sides of the glass as I hand-cranked the paddles.

I liked my Grandma Wright's wooden churn the best. It looked just like a cheerleader's megaphone, big on the bottom with a slender top. It was held together with black metal straps, like a barrel. The top had a lid with a hole in it. What looked like a broomstick was threaded through the hole. Attached to the end of the stick was a round disk that swooshed the milk back and forth as the churner pulled the stick up and down.

You couldn't see the milk once you put the lid on, but with enough practice, you'd know by the feel of the handle when the butter was beginning to coagulate. Even the youngest child could do this job, so it often fell to me, even though I was so short I had to stand up beside the churn and use both hands. I can still feel the ache in my arms from throttling gallons of milk. It's a wonder I didn't grow up lopsided.

When my mind travels back to my childhood, thoughts of food are crowded out by the different venues it took. I marvel at the varieties of food that found their way to the big lion-clawed table. Some came dressed in different coats with a variety of feet ranging from two-legged chickens or geese to four-legged critters, anything from a squirrel or rabbit to a hog, sheep or a cow.

My mouth still waters when I think of how my mother's cracklin' and pone bread smelled when pulled fresh from the oven of a wood stove. We called the cornbread cracklin' bread because it was studded with crusts of crunchy pork fat pieces that Mama had cooked to a crisp and stirred into the raw egg, cornmeal and milk mixture just before baking.

Pone bread was something else altogether. My mother made that in a big red-rimmed white enamel pan. She'd put the flour from the bin into the pan, add salt, soda and shortening, then make a pocket in the flour with her hand. She filled it with buttermilk. The final mixture, a cross between thick pancakes and biscuit batter, was spread out on a baking pan that she'd amply rubbed with bacon grease.

Well, it wasn't really bacon grease. It was "lard" that she'd rendered by cooking hunks of fat cut off a hog's carcass. The fat was cooked, or rendered, in pots over an open fire until it became liquid. The only meat used for rendering were those pieces considered too fatty for the whole hog sausage we also made.

The signal that the bread was ready for baking was when Mama poked holes in the pone with her fingers. That was to let the steam escape, I guess. By the way, pone means a small oval cake, usually made of corn.

Anyway, the finished product had a hard, caramel-colored crust, but the inside was like downy white chicken feathers and was just about as light and airy.

I don't know which was my favorite meal, squirrel gravy and pone bread covered with apple butter or cracklin' bread smeared stem to stern with gobs of real butter. Either one, when accompanied by fresh milk, was wonderful.

But, what was beyond wonderful were the butter cookies and the crullers. The butter cookies were so big that it took both of my hands to hold one of them. I always sat down on the back porch and made sure my dress was pulled tight over my knees before I took the first bite. I'd catch any crumbs on my dress. Even a morsel was too precious to waste.

But, the crullers, well, there was never a chance that a crumb would escape from a cruller. Nosirree. We ate them standing at the stove by my mother's side. Crullers were strange, twisted dough concoctions made from a recipe Mama cut from a magazine. They were fried in boiling lard and tasted something like doughnuts. Most of them never made it to the sugar-dusting stage, because my mother was outnumbered four to one. She couldn't cook the sweet things as fast as we kids could eat them.

But, the sweetest treat of all was the honey and

honeycomb scooped up by the spoonful from the fare provided by my Grandpa Wright's honeybees. Talk about a sugar rush. I still salivate thinking about biting down into the comb and squishing honey on my tongue.

Mama still makes cornbread, but it isn't cracklin' bread. I can't remember when she last made pone bread, but it's been a long time.

She laughed the other day when I told her I was writing about pone bread.

"Be sure you explain what a pone is," she said.

While I can describe what it is and how it was made, the taste, like my memories of it, defies true description.

Your taste buds just had to be there. ≋

May 2000

21

A Word Painter
Discipline needed for the writing life

ONE OF THE BEST THINGS about working at home is that I get to make, as well as break, the rules. If I want to, I can:

1) *sleep late*
2) *read all the newspaper at one sitting*
3) *drink coffee and watch the sunrise*
4) *work in my underwear*
5) *take a break at any time to visit my mama or bake a cake for my daddy*
6) *write a friend or family member a note*
7) *clean house (just kidding)*
8) *procrastinate (this applies only to No. 7)*

Having an office in my home also means that I need to invoke every shred of discipline I can muster and apply it to each new day in order to minimize distractions and stay on schedule while juggling a variety of deadlines.

F. Scott Fitzgerald said, "Writers aren't really

one person; they are a whole lot of people trying to be one person." It makes sense.

I really have a very hard time getting the "writer" person to belly up to a computer when the "sunrise-watching" person is the one standing in front of the kitchen window sipping the second cup of coffee. It's a daily struggle.

When you give it some thought, Fitzgerald had to be right. All writers really must have multiple personalities, some of which are more than a little bit strange. After all, anyone has to be a tad crazy to arrange meetings with perfect strangers, believing that the strangers will then find him instantly trustworthy and begin to divulge dark secrets heretofore told to no one. After all, everybody knows you can trust the press to write "unbiased" stories.

The writer, if he has been convincing enough to pry out a few pertinent facts, then takes several pages of notes. After mulling over the information, for a few hours or days, the writer produces a story that he truly believes will command an audience of thousands simply because he cared enough to sit down and link a few hundred words together on a page. While his work may be read quite often, it also comes in handy for a variety of other uses— like wrapping fish, lining birdcages or catching puppy puddles.

I didn't set out to be a writer. I think my professional career was an accident waiting to happen. By 1979, I had already successfully met my main goal and greatest joy in life, being a wife and a mother of two sons.

I was taking a break from my chosen profession

that summer and was sitting on the porch with my husband, having a glass of iced tea and leisurely reading the *South Hill Enterprise*, one of the local newspapers in Mecklenburg County where my family lived at that time. I handed my husband the classifieds section, which I never read. After a few minutes, he said, "Here's a job for you."

Without even looking up, I replied, "Thank you, but I have two already. They're playing in the sand pile right now."

"Yes, but this is something you already do," he insisted. "It's a writer's job for *The Richmond News Leader.*"

"Have you lost your mind?" I asked.

"Well, you write poetry, don't you?" was the response.

After trying to explain that there was a world of difference between handwritten pencil lines scribbled on a legal pad and being responsible for hard news and local government happenings, my husband remained adamant. In fact, he dared me to go for the interview. He sweetened the offer by betting me $10 that I would get the job as a state correspondent for Mecklenburg, the Virginia county closest to the North Carolina border. I had no aspiration to work outside our home, but a challenge is a challenge. Besides, I planned to win the bet and spend the money on a much-needed haircut.

A week later I went for the interview. Not only did I lose the bet, but my hair stayed long, which pleased my husband immensely. But, I did have to go to work. I was too embarrassed to tell the man who called to congratulate me on getting the job that I really wasn't very interested in it.

Twenty-one years have passed since then, and I'm still writing. Seven years with the newspaper, as well as several other corporate writing jobs in public relations, helped prepare me for my present work as a freelance writer. What an opportunity I would have missed if I hadn't listened to my better half. Without really knowing it, he opened the pathway for something I had never dreamed about.

I had envisioned becoming an artist one day but lacked the necessary financing to develop the skill. Through writing, I have been able to paint word pictures. If I can describe an event, or person with enough meaning and emotion, then the reader can carry the vision around in his mind like a painting he has seen hanging in a gallery.

My husband and I often laughed about how I "fell" into my profession. When I was under deadline pressures, I always groused about how writing wasn't really my "chosen" profession. Somehow it worked out to my advantage, though. I'm not sure I ever thanked Oscar for his inspiration.

My husband died unexpectedly on Sept. 23, 1991. He often comes to mind when I have a tough time getting started on an assignment. After hours, or days, of walking around, grappling for a lead to a story, I hear his quiet voice saying once again, "You can do it."

When I finally get it together and sit down to write, I whisper back, "Thanks, Sugie. This one is for you." ≋

June 2000

22

Degrees of Inspiration
Conspiracy of caring carries this student

Because I was afraid that I couldn't complete requirements for my master's degree, I held off mailing the graduation invitations until I knew I'd passed my oral exams. With only a week to spare, I sent out the invites, with a memo:

TO: *The best family and friends any person could ever have*
FROM: *Nancy Wright Beasley*
DATE: *May 5, 2000*
SUBJ: *Celebration*

About six months ago, I realized that my dream of a graduate degree might truly be in sight. I've been trying since then to think of a way to thank all the people who have stood squarely behind me since I embarked on this venture. Sometimes there are just no words — not even for writers. It seems too inconsequential to just say "thank you" for all the prayers, love and encouragement, phone calls, cards—and in no small way—the monetary support that has inspired and propelled me through these last six and a half years. However, if I had to pick out one person, it would be my mother who was my unfailing inspiration. She has been my guiding light and unwavering support system since before I could walk. She has never stopped believing in my dreams or in me. Without her inspiration and famous, "Nothing beats a failure but a try" saying, which actually came from her mother, I would not have attempted to meet a deadline for a $1,000 National Federation of Press Women scholarship that helped launch this venture. I sent my application by FedEx on the final day of submission, and I remember thinking that I probably didn't have a prayer. Well, I won the scholarship and the rest is now history. Because my mother helped me believe in myself, I had the chutzpah to apply for other scholarships.

As I walk down that aisle next Saturday, I will be only a singular person but there will be a crowd around me, as well as a few angels looking on. I can only say that each and every one of you has helped me in ways that you can't imagine. For that, I am so grateful. For that, I will attempt to become the best writer I can be, always remembering whose shoulders I'm standing on.

I immediately framed my degree and propped it on a chair in the living room so that I could see it every day. Sometimes at night, I'd fix a cup of coffee and just sit next to it, marveling at its mere existence. I kept remembering different incidents that helped me plow through the maze. Two times in particular kept coming to mind.

It's been so long since the first one that I can't remember the year. My younger son, Jason, then a student at Coastal Carolina University in South Carolina, was expected home for Christmas. I had my hands in the sink washing vegetables when he entered the house. Before I could even speak or turn around, he asked, "What's wrong, Mom?" Jason has always been able to tell when something is bothering me.

I explained that, although I had worked diligently, I just couldn't get the hang of writing a 15-page paper. The deadline was looming.

"Well, what's your thesis statement?" he asked. When I said, "I'm not sure I have one," he just rolled his eyes and said, "Show me what information you have."

Even though he had just polished off several research papers himself, he sat down at my computer. When I offered information, he put up his hand and said, "I'll let you know when I need help."

I retreated to the sink again deciding to rely on yet another of my Mama's famous sayings: "Beggars can't be choosers."

He finally announced, "There's good news and bad news. The good news is that this paper is salvageable. The bad news is that you don't have nearly enough sources to make a cogent argument for your subject."

I turned off the stove. He grabbed our jackets. We emerged from Cabell Library at midnight, starving but euphoric in our discovery of information. It took most of my son's vacation and several shouting matches before he could convince his mother, the veteran writer in the family, that there is a huge chasm between writing for the public and writing for scholars. I finally learned that the latter doesn't necessarily have to make sense to the former.

The second incident involves my older son and his wife.

During the last six months of school, days and nights melded, as writing deadlines and project completions collided with my aging parents' doctors' appointments. I thought constantly of giving up, or at least putting off graduation until December.

Late one night, I was considering the possibility of taking a sabbatical from classes. After discussing this option with Beau, he said, "Leila and I have been thinking. We know you're having a tough time and we thought you needed an incentive. We've decided to give you our vacation week at Barrier Island Station as a graduation present, because we know you're going to make it—in May."

Talk about incentive. To me, heaven on earth is a private beach and eating fresh seafood. When I arrived at Duck, N.C., to find a furnished apartment where I could watch the sun go down and hear the ocean, I felt as if I had reached paradise.

There's a good explanation why a fire for education burns inside me. My 86-year-old father is illiterate and my 80-year-old mother was forced to quit school at age 12 to help her family survive the Depression. They drove home the message of getting an education to the point that it dominated the life lessons of all four of their children. The question was not "if" my siblings and I were going to college, but "where" we were going. While all of us attended college, I'm the only one who decided to make it a lifelong career.

I was 39 before I completed my undergraduate degree. My husband was 42. Oscar graduated the same year Beau received his high school diploma. For seven years running, some, or all four, members of our family were in school at the same time.

Thirty-seven years lapsed between my high school graduation and May 13, the day I accepted my master's degree from Dr. Clarence W. Thomas, the director of graduate studies at the Virginia Commonwealth University School of Mass Communications.

Dr. Thomas was another "giant" whom I leaned on consistently. He was relentless in his support. At times, he seemed more certain than I was that I would attain my lifelong dream. He kept saying, "You can do this. I have faith in you. You just have to keep trying."

If I didn't know better, I'd think he conspired with my Mama. ≋

September 2000

23

Hair of Maturity
Stylist calms hair-raising predicaments

"No. 89 IS SPIKING," Les Blackwell said to me as we faced each other in a serious discussion.

"I know, I know," I replied in exasperation, "but at least No. 36 has leveled out. On the other hand, Nos. 23 and 15 seem to be going completely flat. What do you think? Should we invest in a totally different direction, cut back or just stay the course?"

While our conversation sounded much like a stock market discourse, it was actually a discussion my hair stylist instigated recently when I was having a particularly bad hair day.

After Les nearly pulled his own blonde hair out while trying to find a hairstyle for me that we both could live with, I came up with the system of assigning numbers to errant patches of my disheveled mane. It took lots and lots of patience on Les's part before we ever truly agreed. When I arrive at his salon now, he just grins and asks, "The usual?"

I just don't get it. I keep wondering where the naturally wavy auburn hair I was born with is hiding. I long for its return. Les, bless his more realistic heart, prefers to say, "I think gray hair is attractive on a mature woman."

Never mind that my head of quickly graying hair has a mind of its own. While I was originally endowed with very thick, manageable locks, something former hair stylists have oohed and aahed over each time they started to cut my hair, now the two cowlicks lurking at the border of my scalp have decided to create hair havoc.

For the city slicker reading this, a cowlick is the country description of one part of a person's hair that has an unnaturally swept-up look, kinda like when a cow licks you in the face, starting just above the outside corner of your eye and ending across your forehead, which leaves the wet hair standing on end. Remember Alfalfa on the Little Rascals? Like Alfalfa, I have two cowlicks, one in the front and one in the back. I inherited them from my Mama. Had to. My Daddy is bald.

At 55, my cowlicks have taken over and just can't wait to spring up at any unpredictable moment. In former, as in younger, days, I could arise from bed and my hair was never mussed. After pajama parties, my teenage girlfriends would ask me if I had slept standing up. Now, one of my greatest fears is having my fire alarm go off in the middle of the night. I can just envision it. I'd be standing barefoot in the front yard in a gown before I realized that I had vacated my premises without slathering down the spikes on my head. Since my hair has started to "mature," as Les calls it, I have begun to look exactly like Groucho Marx when I get up in the morning.

I'm thinking of investing in some Wild Root Creme Oil Charlie. Again, for city slickers, that's an old-timey (I know the correct way is "old-time," but I like my word better. That's the way "true" country folks say it.) version of hair tonic that mountain men used when they were trying to plaster down their sun-baked hair. Women, on the other hand, used a lotion called Suave. If you're not old enough to remember those radio commercials, you probably wouldn't remember the Burma-Shave signs posted along the highway either, so I won't even go there. But, shaving my head is one option I've seriously considered recently.

I don't know what I ever did to deserve Les or his vigilant care. Actually, I think it has more to do with his loyalty to my oldest sister, Janet Watkins. When I moved to Richmond, I had to find a local hairdresser. Since my sis's hair always looked so chic, naturally I asked who did the styling. She heartily endorsed Les, since he had been cutting her hair for nigh unto 15 years by then. While Les recently gave my sister a Susan Powter cut that looks wonderful on her, he hasn't been brave enough to suggest it for me.

Boy, was I ever surprised when I saw Les the first time. I don't know what I was expecting, but the good-looking 6-foot, broad-shouldered guy with a full beard wasn't it. With a quiet demeanor and the calmness of a surgeon, he picked up his styling scissors and snipped away. After the initial visit, I learned that you don't tell Les you "really" want a hair cut. While my hair was styled beautifully, most of it was also missing.

I growled, paid him and returned six weeks later hoping to convince him to leave a little fuzz. He did.

Over the last six years, I have grown to deeply appreciate Les and his careful attentiveness. He not only styles my hair, which becomes magically transformed under his gentle hands, he also asks about my family members and actually listens to the answers. We discuss political persuasions, religion, our children and the states of health of both our elderly mothers. In fact, going to see Les is more like a time of friendship; however, I don't pay my other friends as well.

Just about the time we really got used to each other, Les decided to up and move his business, Les & Company Hair Design, from Jefferson Davis Highway to a larger location in downtown Chester, Va. It took me every bit of five seconds to make a similar decision to follow him. Never mind that a haircut now necessitates a 34-mile trek from home and back. It really doesn't matter too much. The extra time gives me a few minutes to start relaxing before I see Les, something I'm sure he is thankful for. Sometimes, though, the mellowness wears off in our discussions over No. 89. She is a particularly hardheaded, bristly hair. We've learned over time to just ignore her.

She doesn't go away, but then, neither do "mature" women. ≋

October 2000

24

Looking Back with Gratitude at Christmas
Joy of family and friends sets holiday tone

I ALWAYS SEEM TO WAKE ESPECIALLY EARLY on Christmas Day, probably a carry-over from times past when there were two little boys eagerly waiting to raid the Christmas bounty.

My older son, Beau, and his wife, Leila, spent the night with me last Christmas Eve. I had yielded my bed, since I'm the only one short enough to sleep comfortably on the couch. Sun streaming through the bay window in the den woke me a little earlier than usual, so I started the coffee and tiptoed out to get the morning paper. As I settled in to read the front page, I started crying. Not because it was the last Christmas Day of the millennium, but because I was overcome with joy.

I rejoiced because I had just walked onto my frost-covered yard with the assurance that the *Richmond Times-Dispatch* would be waiting. Because there were people who had worked really hard, just like they do every day of the year, to produce that newspaper. And, because there are writers like Mark Holmberg whose prose reminded me once again in a front page story that there are folks who keep on working when the rest of us either slow down or come to a complete standstill.

Mark's story last Christmas Day was about two Richmond men, Harry Ragland and Raymond Mormon, employees of the Richmond Department of Refuse Collection. The article described their arduous, and primarily thankless, job of collecting trash on Christmas Eve, which was business as usual for them. Because of individuals like Ragland and Mormon, we can enjoy a fuss-free holiday, knowing that, starting all over again tomorrow, they, and others just like them, will be on the job making sure that our world keeps poking along on schedule.

I rejoiced because the day before I found a cake on my front porch left there by my neighbors, Rick and Beth Wolfe. A piece of green paper, cut out like a Christmas tree and stuck to the cake, held this message: "Amish Loaf from the Wolfes. Freezes well if you don't need it now."

I rejoiced because of the wonder of the world and the sheer beauty of waking up another morning; because I could go to a church that day, or any day, and not fear government reprisal; because I was healthy and could walk and see and hear.

I rejoiced because my children have not disappointed me. Beau and Jason would both be home, where it's okay to eat chocolate covered peanuts in the middle of the day, or the middle of the night for that matter, and where it's okay to laugh a little too loud, leave the house at odd times or make long distance phone calls and worry about the cost tomorrow.

Because I was reared in more austere surroundings, I thought my late husband was crazy when he started planning the Christmas decorations in August each year. As the Christmas season approached, there was always at least one disaster and lots of laughter as we ceremoniously went through the woods choosing a tree. Inevitably, the tree would be so large that it would hang over the sides and extend beyond the top of the F100 he dubbed "Old Blue."

In my parents' home, you might sneak presents in the back door, but you certainly didn't dress up in Santa outfits and plan parties for the grandchildren like my in-laws did. It was all a mismatch in my mind anyway, my being a child and an adult at the same time, until I finally realized that being childlike is how you survive in this world of hard knocks.

Traditions are why we come home at Christmas or on any holiday. It's the glue that holds the family in a central place. Computers may speed up our world, but they will never replace the wonder in a child's eyes when seeing a live Nativity scene for the first time or hanging up a stocking in anticipation.

2000 will be the second year of a new tradition for me. I'll be rejoicing when I thread about a zillion tiny, white lights around the wrought iron railing of my front porch. Sensing that I was a little blue last year, my sister, Janet, handed me two large boxes of lights and said, "Here, you deserve some light in your life." The present was especially meaningful because she had managed the shopping on tottering legs. Two plastic knees, installed only three months earlier, still caused her to walk like Frankenstein's monster.

Those lights will continue to shine for many more Christmases and have special meaning, just like the card Janet sent me in 1988. I unpacked it year after year, until I finally decided to frame and display it. Now, when I see the bright green frame shining up at me from among the Christmas paraphernalia, it takes me back to when I stood in my driveway and read it for the first time. I'm still moved with the simplicity and beauty of what Henry Van Dyke wrote so many years ago. He must have written it to a special friend and it got passed along to others before it finally became a greeting card.

This year, I'd like to share it with you, my faithful friends and readers, who take the time to call or write a note and say you appreciate this column. I hope you enjoy the verse and pass it along to someone special. Van Dyke wrote:

> *I am thinking of you today because it is Christmas, and I wish you happiness. And tomorrow, because it will be the day after Christmas, I shall still wish you happiness. My thoughts and my wishes will be with you always. Whatever joy comes to you will make me glad. All through the year, I wish you the spirit of Christmas.* ≋

December 2000

25

Gone But Not Forgotten
Aunt's death is a reminder to live

THE YEAR 2000 WAS significant, not just because it was the first year of a new century, but because one of the brightest lights in my family went out. When the phone rang at 4:40 a.m. on Nov. 5, I hesitated before answering it, knowing full well that whoever was calling had to be facing some kind of turmoil.

When I heard my cousin's quiet voice, I could tell she was crying. Not really wanting to know the answer, I asked, "Ruthie, have we lost Aunt Dorothy?"

Dorothy Krivanec, 76, a native Virginian who moved to Jacksonville, Fla., several years ago, was what most people would refer to as a "pistol." No one, especially her children, was ever quite sure what to expect from her. Saying she was a "character" or "spirited" certainly describes some of her attributes, but it doesn't quite do her justice. Dorothy was a little bit like a skunk, absolutely beautiful to look at, but somewhat dangerous to touch at times.

I remember watching her as a child and thinking she was almost magic. When she was tickled, she would throw her head back, give her long red mane a shake and let out a belly laugh that encompassed everybody in the room. Her mischievous manner affected anyone even remotely close to her. It was impossible to be sad around her for more than a few minutes. Regardless of where Aunt Dorothy was, you could always count on a commotion of one kind or other going on.

My aunt was 11 years younger than my father and was the last surviving daughter in a family of 12. She grew up near a little town called Christiansburg, Va., during the "hard" times, between the Great Depression and World War II, before inside toilets and electricity became part of everyday life and about the time that school attendance was mandated by the state.

As a teenager, my aunt married a raven-haired man named Roy Dove. She gave birth to two daughters and a son before divorcing him and subsequently marrying a few more times. She eventually outlived two other husbands and her youngest daughter, Susie. My aunt told me recently that she had finally decided she was finished with marriage and planned to dedicate her last years to going to yard sales, refurbishing the clothes she found there and reselling them. She did buy a lot of things, but managed to give away even more.

Aunt Dorothy's older daughter, Ruth Ann Turner, and her husband, Herbert, would bring my aunt to visit my parents over the years. It was a long trip from Jacksonville to Richmond. They'd usually leave at 3 a.m. and drive all day. It never marred Aunt Dorothy's delight in the visit. She might say she had a "little" arthritis, but she would jump up to help put food on the table or relinquish her chair to anyone who entered the house.

My aunt never came to visit without presents. Just a few weeks before her death she brought my mother, her favorite sister-in-law, a brand-new, beautiful, warm robe for the winter. My Daddy got shirts from the yard-sale trove, the same place my new grass-cutting shoes came from. Aunt Dorothy took great delight in passing along her "treasures."

For the last several years, she lived near Ruth Ann, Herbert and Roy Jr., whom we all refer to as Jingle. They were with her when she died a few hours after suffering a massive stroke. I couldn't help thinking she died like she lived—in a streak and a fury, leaving a tumultuous path behind.

The path she left can't be walked by anyone else. While she was an ornery, irascible, opinionated, and often frustrating person, she was completely genuine and would always come down on the side of understanding. As my sister, Janet, said, "You instinctively knew that everything she felt was from her heart. When she looked into your eyes and talked to you, it was understood that she had given you the attention of her entire soul."

When the family closed ranks for her memorial service, there were more than a few passing references to Aunt Dorothy's antics. Ruth Ann always referred to her mother as a "mess" with a loving tone in her voice. My aunt had that effect on anyone she met. Regardless of her antics, she somehow got away with them and managed to earn people's respect to boot. There's one story about how she shot out all four tires on a car because she wanted to talk to the driver who was ignoring her. The story goes that she stood on a porch near a milking barn and picked off those tires, one at a time, until the car stopped. I'm sure the man was more than ready to talk by the fourth blowout.

My Daddy recalls that when he and Aunt Dorothy attended the funeral of their older sister, Laura, about nine months ago, they both enjoyed a sweet moment reminiscing about how Laura, the quiet one, was always being pulled into trouble by Dorothy during their childhood days.

While Dorothy did seem to enjoy stirring up things, she was also a stalwart woman who could comfort, even though I never saw her shed a tear. When she left my parents' home for the last time, she lovingly hugged my mother and then my Daddy in a rougher manner. While Daddy and I fought back tears, she jauntily walked down the steps like a teenager before looking back for a final time, winking and saying, "What are y'all crying about? Everything is going to be all right."

I've decided to take that advice to heart in the New Year. I plan to emulate my aunt's love of life and her overwhelmingly positive attitude. I'm going to laugh more often and find more humor in everyday life. I've made a New Year's resolution in her honor to visit the people I love frequently and take them gifts.

But, I doubt I'll be shooting out any tires. 〰

January 2001

26

Remembrance of Things Past
William Styron's *Sophie* brings home the Holocaust

IT WAS, BY ANYONE'S STANDARDS, A star-studded evening. Women dripped diamonds and furs, while men were relegated to their usual monochromatic formal attire. Wine flowed and hands were clasped as Richmond's elite craned their necks to see the rich and famous who had come to the Library of Virginia to help crown the new statewide reading program.

All Virginia Reads, a year-long emphasis on one particular book by a Virginia author, was devoted to William Styron in 2000. Styron, a Newport News son before becoming author extraordinaire, was being honored for *Sophie's Choice*, a novel he wrote in 1979.

Although the event culminated at the state library, it was the beautiful swan song of a huge joint effort encompassing the Virginia Center for the Book, the Library of Virginia Foundation and numerous program partners and corporate sponsors. The main goal of the projects was to foster renewed interest in reading across the commonwealth, promote books and excellence in literature and begin a statewide dialogue about indifference, intolerance, hatred and injustice.

Sophie's Choice is the story of Sophie Zawistowska, a Polish-Catholic Holocaust survivor living in New York City with her lover, Nathan Landau. As narrated by Stingo, an aspiring writer fresh to New York from college, Sophie's account of life at Auschwitz, a concentration camp in Poland, unfolds, intertwining with Nathan's jealous brutality and Stingo's growing infatuation with Sophie.

Although Sophie manages to survive, she is plagued by a decision she is forced to make. The climax of the story centers on a scene where Sophie realizes that she must make an impossible choice, whether to surrender her son or her daughter to be killed by the Nazis.

During the tribute to Styron, there were few references to the scars left by the Holocaust, which is so vividly captured through Meryl Streep's portrayal of Sophie in the book's movie rendition under the brilliant producer Alan Pakula.

Pakula was killed suddenly in an accident about two years ago. His widow, Hannah, a historical author, attended the event honoring Styron. Kevin Kline, who played the supporting role opposite Streep, paid tribute to Pakula's insight into the work and offered a toast in his memory.

The evening ended with a musical tribute by Bruce Hornsby, who let his fingers dance across the Baldwin piano.

For some unknown reason, I began to visualize the musicians who were forced to play as their friends and family members marched past them to the gas chambers more than 60 years ago. I watched while remnants of unwanted food, originally served to us on gold-rimmed plates, were removed to be thrown away. It was a far cry from newsreels in the 1940s that captured human beings fighting for scraps of bread.

I looked over the crowd, trying to find Gertrude Kupfer. During the cocktail hour, Kupfer had stood quietly with her hands folded in front of her, not even having a drink. She blended into the crowd, hardly noticed among hundreds who did their best to elbow a turn to meet stars like Mike Wallace and Diane Sawyer, celebrity newscasters and friends of Styron's. No one would have guessed that Kupfer, a diminutive white-haired woman who probably weighs less than 100 pounds, was a Holocaust survivor.

I met Kupfer about four years ago, when I first began writing about survivors who live in Richmond, Va. I remember recounting the difficulty of the work to my sister Janet. Like most people, my sister prefers to read about brighter subjects.

Janet seemed particularly exasperated with me one day when I was recounting the sadness of writing about such things and asked, "Why are you doing this if it hurts you so much? Do you think you are the conscience of the whole world?" At the time, I didn't answer her, but I did ponder the question.

After the library event, where the virtues of Styron's work were hailed, I now understand more fully why writers and scholars were some of the first to be eliminated during the Holocaust scourge that wiped out several million lives. Writers and artists see things in a different light and reflect those events as truthfully as possible through their work. Sometimes, we dare to peel back the layers of the human onion and expose places that don't look so palatable in the light. We don't especially enjoy that part of our work. The mere action hurts us as well, but we are compelled to do it just the same.

I couldn't sleep the night after the library affair. The fact that books surrounded us was not lost on me. One of the first things the Nazis did was to burn books they found offensive. They not only burned works by Einstein, one of the targeted Jews, they also burned Hemingway, Fitzgerald and even Helen Keller, the latter because any individual who was limited either physically or mentally was considered unworthy of a role in the life of the perfect Aryan nation the Nazis envisioned.

Meryl Streep said playing the role of Sophie changed her life. She was careful, however, to differentiate between playing the character, which she said she immediately abandoned after the film was complete, and the fact that Styron was able to actually embody the character of Sophie and bring her to life through his words.

Styron's words also had a profound effect on Jack Spiro, retired rabbi of Congregation Beth Ahabah and the Harry Lyons distinguished professor in the Department of Religious Studies at Virginia Commonwealth University.

Before offering a blessing for the meal, Spiro

recounted memories of a meeting he had with Styron some 20 years earlier. During an interview that was to be aired on public radio, the rabbi asked Styron if there was an underlying theme running through all of his novels.

"I guess he took me by surprise when he said, 'Yes,'" Spiro recalled. "His answer was both unpretentious and profound. He said, 'The theme is that the greatest of all evils is the domination of one human being by another.'" The rabbi said those words became a mantra, never to be forgotten.

Because words have such power, it makes sense that the Nazis would have burned books. Authors not only question authority and let their work reflect the time in which they live, they leave records for others to read and learn from.

In that way, writers are, indeed, the conscience of the whole world. ≋

March 2001

27

Shall We Gather at the River?
Baptism unites all

THE DAY COULDN'T make up its mind. Cotton-candy clouds had vied with a gray sky all morning. Continous rumblings of far-away thunder cast doubts on the upcoming event causing more than a little chagrin for the waiting participants. Entering water with lightning in the background would definitely be an act of faith.

My younger son, Jason, sat nervously amid a group of worshipers gathered at the boat landing of Robious Landing Park looking more like he was dressed for a beach party instead of a baptism. He was chewing gum as if his life depended on it.

A married couple and a lone man had stepped into the water first, after sharing their reasons for committing to a Christian life. They had read from index cards, referring to favorite Scriptures or times in their lives when they had needed a higher power. They rose, dripping with water and anticipation of their new lease on life. As the third participant was submerged, a boat passed in the background, causing waves to cascade across each other and raising the water level to waist high on Jim Dowdy, the officiating pastor.

In slow motion, a man steered the boat while a woman trailed her hands in the warm water. They were probably the parents of the little boy riding in an inner tube tethered to the boat by a long rope. Although the child was almost hidden in a spray of water, his enjoyment was enunciated by the pumping of his feet turned skyward. His legs looked like flexible straws protruding from a foamy drink. The ease of the lad's life at that moment reminded me of the turmoil my son had sometimes faced when he was young.

Born to a chronically ill father, Jason had probably been tossed and turned by life more than most youngsters during his era. His understanding of life was no doubt clouded by thoughts of diabetes intertwined with Nintendo or Pac-Man. That little yellow, moon-faced guy had eaten a path through Jason's psyche while he was very young and had given him a penchant for all things electronic.

Now my broad-shouldered son, almost 31, a computer systems engineer and black-belt jujitsu instructor, was sitting on a riverbank contemplating the meaning of life and looking nervous as a cat about to be dunked in a bubble bath. He had called the day before to tell me of the event. The conversation went something like this.

"Hi, Mom. Whatcha doin'?"

"I'm cleaning kitchen cabinets. What are you doing?"

"Well, I wanted to see if you would be busy

tomorrow."

"That depends. What do you need?"

"I've decided to be baptized. I thought you might want to come."

"Baptized?" I asked. "Weren't you baptized once already?"

"Yes, but I was so young. I don't think I really understood the commitment."

"Do you now?"

"Well, let's put it this way. I don't know if I can do it. I have to make a public profession of faith, and you know how nervous I get when I have to speak in front of people."

"Yes, I understand. But, you can do it."

And do it he did.

When his turn came, he stood uneasily. The action of his jaws pumping the chewing gum resembled a fireman stoking a steam engine.

"I'm sorry," he started. "My Mama said I should spit this gum out before speaking. But, my mouth is so dry right now, I need it. I'm just not a public speaker. I don't have any Scriptures to refer to. I'll just talk from my heart," he said waving both hands in the air. Suddenly aware of his floating appendages, he explained, "I can't talk without using my hands. I must be half-Italian." Then he quickly added, "No offense to any Italians who might be here."

The next words were sometimes audible and sometimes muffled by emotion. He paid homage to his early Christian training and explained that those childhood lessons went the way of the surf for a while at Myrtle Beach, a place where he said "nobody should go to college."

He quietly continued, "My Mom is here but unfortunately...." His voice trailed off. He just couldn't bring himself to say that he father was dead. In the momentary silence, I'm sure many of the witnesses were having thoughts like mine.

It was Father's Day, a day when families honor men for the many hours of toil and unseen sacrifices they make for their loved ones. I thought of my husband, Oscar, and wished he were present to witness the depth and stability that Jason has found. The event had already taken on special significance when, prior to the baptisms, the church members began spontaneously singing *Amazing Grace* the same song that a bagpiper played at the end of my husband's memorial service.

While Christianity may not be the answer to everyone's spiritual needs, Grace Bible Church has become a haven for my son. Since his father's death in 1991, Jason has seemed like a boat adrift at times. Now he has found an anchor amidst the tumbles of life and feels that he is accepted, chewing gum and all.

When Jim lifted Jason from the water, they embraced for a long time. It reminded me of when my husband would come home after a hard day's work. The first thing he did was find our two boys and hug them.

Jason and his Dad had found a new depth of love and respect for each other the summer before Oscar died. That's why the ensuing years have been so hard for Jason. I'm sure he still misses the bear hugs that he had grown accustomed to over the years.

Standing on that riverbank I realized that my son had gained a whole new family. Although his natural father was physically absent, he was with us in a very tangible way.

As I walked up the bank, a gentle rain began to fall. I could have sworn I heard Oscar say, "Amen." ≋

June 2001

28

Sisisky: Congressman, Patriot
At funeral, friends remember man who made a difference

"When you teach your son, you teach your son's son."
– Talmud

CALL ME OLD SCHOOL, BUT I always get choked up on the Fourth of July. I'm a dyed-in-the-wool patriot, proud of the fact that I learned the Pledge of Allegiance as a schoolgirl. I still stand to recite it with my hand over my heart when an American flag is hoisted at some special occasion. I was overcome with that same feeling recently.

It was a rainy April day. There were so many colorful umbrellas unfurled on Grove Avenue it looked like spring flowers popping up midway of the sidewalk. In actuality, it was a somber throng of people making their way to Temple Beth-El quietly waiting their turn to enter the beige, stained glass-studded synagogue. They had come to pay their last respects to Norman Sisisky. A son of immigrants, Sisisky, was the first Jewish congressman to be elected from Virginia. He began his political career in the Virginia General Assembly in 1973, where he served for almost 10 years. A Democrat, he went on to Congress in 1982 and represented the Fourth District until his death.

Although the synagogue seats about 500, there was standing room only that Sunday. I only saw one unoccupied seat, left vacant because folks coming by twos and threes needed to stay together to comfort one another.

I had known Norman for a long time, probably close to 20 years. I knew a lot about him, but I didn't know he was Jewish until a couple of years ago, when I moved back to Richmond and also learned that, by marriage, he was part of the local Brown Distributing Company heritage whose original wellspring began from Lithuanian immigrant roots.

My remembrances of Norman were chock-full with memories of his never-failing support of our armed forces. He might have wavered on other issues, but never this one. He fought like the bulldog he resembled to keep military bases not only open but viable places to live, work and flourish. He understood the importance because he, like so many of the "Greatest Generation," was a veteran of the Navy, having served as a teenager during World War II.

Fighting must have been in his blood. Otherwise, why would he have wanted to become a congressman? Although it's not a very fun place to work, Norman seemed to thrive in the brutal D.C. atmosphere. Perhaps it was because he was independently wealthy and really didn't need the job. Perhaps it was because he knew he was filling a "minority" spot. Perhaps it was because he believed he could truly make a difference in someone's life. Sitting among the mourners, I realized that he had made a difference in mine.

As I listened to tributes offered by several dignitaries, I thought back a few years to the times when I acted as a chaperone for Southside Virginia teenagers involved with the National Rural Electric Cooperative Association Youth Tour. The various electric cooperatives in Virginia, Maryland and Delaware that comprise the Old Dominion Electric Cooperative, their parent organization, have been sending about 100 teens to Washington, D.C., to learn about the history of rural electrification and the part that government played in its early development for almost 30 years. When I previously lived in South Hill and worked for Mecklenburg Electric Cooperative, I escorted several youth groups to Washington. The four-day trip was always packed with events, including a full day spent on The Hill calling on national representatives. I'll never forget that, while other politicians didn't always find the time to meet with the teens, Norman never turned us down. Not only that, he was always punctual. The one time that he was late, he called ahead to be sure his assistant served Virginia peanuts for us to munch on while waiting.

Norman was a big man with huge hands and a stare-you-down look, but his demeanor was softened by an ever-present smile. He'd come into the room, shake each young person's hand, ask where they were from and what their aspirations were. He never sat behind his mammoth desk, but preferred instead to lean on the edge so he could be close to the group. He never failed to encourage them to "vote and get involved in politics, because you can make a difference." And, he always mentioned the military and how proud he was to serve on the Senate Armed Services Committee.

Speakers at Norman's funeral all testified to that fact and how he was able to benefit the military through his congressional service. Numerous stories — some funny, some somber — were shared. The final speaker was Mark Sisisky, the oldest of Norman and Rhoda's four sons. As Mark cleared his throat and gathered his courage, a deeper quiet fell across the room. When he began to speak, it was with great effort. Was it hard? You bet. Did he stumble with emotion? Unquestionably. Did he, like his father, rise to the occasion? Without a doubt. The words that the younger Sisisky spoke rang out like a bell tolling the times in his father's life that had meant so much to him and his family. Mark reverently spoke each grandchild's name, finding a way to reflect his father's best heritage, that of family.

As he stood there, I couldn't help but think of Norman and how proud he would be of his son. As Mark turned to embrace the rabbi and reclaim his seat, it was obvious that the branch had not fallen very far from the tree.

Norman would have liked that. He would have liked the fact that the last word spoken was by a family member and encompassed loved ones. He would have liked the fact that those in attendance could take home a beautiful personal tribute, aside from his other accomplishments. He would have also liked the fact that there were high-ranking military officers standing at attention as he left for his final journey.

As honorary pallbearers lined up, friends and relatives rose to their feet out of respect. There were so many people between me and the center aisle that I could only see the flag-draped casket through elbows. Without any thought to the motion, I slowly placed my hand over my heart as the casket rolled by. The red, white and blue stood out against the dark clothes that most folks chose to wear that day. Somehow that was fitting too.

Norman was dressed in his finest. ≋

July 2001

29

And a Little Child Shall Lead Them
Lessons learned from frogs
and a little boy

About twice a year, I head for the beach to work. Honest. While I enjoy walking on the sand at sunrise, I can forego other activities. The ocean is the one place where I've discovered I can get quiet and write succinctly.

Aiming for a chapter on a book I've been writing, I headed for Barrier Island Station in Duck, NC, over the Memorial Day weekend.

The first morning I rose eagerly to watch the sunrise. The ritual stays the same. Fix the coffee pot the night before so I can punch the "on" button while I'm dressing. By the time I've grabbed the coffee, a book and hit the beach, the sun is just breaking over the horizon. I usually watch the sun dance off the incoming tide and scan the horizon for porpoises while deciding on a work theme for the day.

Four sunrises came and went. No word was forthcoming. The only thing I really accomplished was sleeping a lot—night and day—and reading a newly purchased book. By the fifth day, I was ready to pull my hair out. Not only was I stymied; I was so frustrated by not writing that I couldn't even relax and enjoy being at the beach. Try as I might, I was unable to break through the months-long writer's block I'd been experiencing. On the sixth day, I threw in the towel and went to Manteo, a nearby town, for a street festival. I figured if I couldn't write, I could at least support the local artisans and volunteer fire departments.

On my last morning I overslept and missed the sunrise.

"That figures," I muttered out loud. Sulking, I went to the gazebo where I always go, still hoping for some last-day breakthrough. I opened the book I had purchased to help me out of the writing slump. Its title, *Eat That Frog*, was an explanation that all tasks should be viewed as frogs. In order to succeed in a day, or for a lifetime, the author proposed that the biggest, nastiest frog with the most warts, i.e., the hardest task, had to be eaten first every day. The premise wasn't new to me; in fact, eating a frog seemed almost tame to the week I'd just had.

Engrossed in the book, I didn't see the little boy dressed in blue jelly sandals and a man's white shirt until he was standing beside me. When I looked up, he raised both hands, made circles with his fingers and placed them to his eyes, as if to mirror my large-framed glasses.

"Whatcha reading?" he asked.

"A book on frogs," I replied.

He stepped closer with interest.

Thinking he was too little to read, I asked, "Can

you find the word 'frog' on this page?"

"It starts with a 'Fr..', right? I don't see it."

I took off my glasses in jest and offered them to him. He balanced them on his nose, looked at his father very seriously and then began to peruse the page again.

"I still don't see it."

I helped him find the word and then explained the "frog" premise. He listened with intensity.

"What's your name?" I asked.

"Alexander. What's yours?"

I told him and then I couldn't wait any longer.

"Alexander, I just have to ask. Why are you wearing a long shirt to the beach?"

"Shirt," he scoffed incredulously. "This is a lab coat."

I didn't dare laugh.

"Does that mean you are a scientist?"

"Of course."

"Well, you must have something of a scientific nature in that Winnie the Pooh backpack, right?"

As I watched, my tiny new friend quickly began to unearth his treasures. He presented me with a green plastic microscope and then explained how he used it to study specimens. He also produced an odd-looking purple and clear gadget, for studying insects without hurting them. A little dump truck was followed by a rock.

With a very solemn 5-year-old face, Alexander explained that he carried the rock with him to remind him of home, just in case he got homesick. The final draw from the pack was a green rubber butterfly and a bright red curlicue bracelet with a large skeleton key attached to it.

"You see this key," he said. "It's the key to the condo."

"Condo?"

His father had to clarify.

"It's the key to the Congo. Alexander plans to go there some day."

"Alexander, are you going to be a scientist in the Congo?" I asked.

"Of course. Do you know how to measure sine waves? I'm going to grow up and study sine waves. C'mon Mrrzzssusss. Beasley, let's go."

Unable to refrain, I kicked off my shoes and followed Alexander and his father, Isaac Sahhar, to the wet sand. Alexander immediately discovered a gull feather, which he in turn tickled my nose with and then squatted to draw sine waves and explain how they were measured by drawing a median line through their peaks and valleys. He took turns studying and then chasing sand crabs, dodging waves and turning over shells, punctuating the air continuously with questions and "Zap," his favorite word.

I learned that he likes to take things apart — mostly radios. He stopped long enough to explain that his nearly yellow and green skin around his left eye was the result of a spring releasing too fast from a radio frame that he had dismantled recently. He also explained that Mommy was sleeping in on their last day of vacation, that she was a former school teacher who stayed at home to teach him and that she always needed a break about the time Daddy got home from his job as a systems engineer. And, no, he wasn't interested in being interviewed, but he'd like me to visit him sometime, since we both lived in Richmond, Va., south of the James.

By necessity, my work week ended right there in mid-visit. I took my leave and slowly walked back to begin the checkout process. I wasn't so depressed any more. I watched Alexander as he continued to dart to and fro on the sand with his backpack. I looked at my book and thought I could have saved my money if I had just met him earlier in the week.

Alexander didn't need instructions. He knew exactly where he was going, was dressed for the job and had a backpack loaded for the trip—a microscope for discovery, a rock for security and parents who loved him and were supporting his belief in his abilities. With a key to the Congo, there is no doubt in my mind that Alexander will make it. I'm going to keep his name and number handy.

I plan to call him the next time I get discouraged and need a role model. ≋

September 2001

30

When Love Hurts
How the domestic violence project began

It's 4:45 a.m. and I'm eating double chocolate ice cream, super-chunk peanut butter and a banana. It's not breakfast, but comfort food that I instinctively reach for when I need courage. I've spent the last six months trying to decide whether to write this column. Last night was the clincher. I woke hours ago with my arms and hands covering my head, as if to ward off the words. When I finally arose, there was no doubt it had to go on paper.

I thought my parents would both have to be deceased before I could write about my father beating my mother. That it would be too humiliating, too hard to explain to friends and relatives who either simply couldn't, or would choose not to, believe it. I wondered how I'd face my three siblings knowing that I was publicly pulling the scab from a very deep, private wound that we've never discussed.

It all began last year when Eric Norbom, a local photographer, called Susan Winiecki, editor of *Richmond Magazine*. Eric was looking for a journalist to work with him on a book about domestic violence and sexual assault. Susan suggested me. Initially, I was afraid of it but my childhood experience kept nudging me toward it.

Just two weeks before my mother died, I finally got the nerve to tell her that I had undertaken the work. She spoke very quietly, but she might as well have been using a megaphone. She shook her head a little and said, "You won't have any trouble getting copy for that." The ensuing research proved her right and developed into this special report.

I must've been about 4 the first time I remember my mother being beaten. I distinctly remember riding in a car going to a hospital. My father's employer, one of the richest and most influential men in Richmond, Va., was driving. I don't remember much except that my mother's face was bleeding profusely and I had to sit in the emergency room for a long time waiting for her. The memory ends there, as if cut off in midstream.

The next time it picks up, I'm standing in the front yard with my mother a couple of years later in the dead of night. This time we were living in Christiansburg, Va., on my father's family farm. My mother had run naked into the yard. My father had ripped off her clothes as she fled trying to avoid his fists. While attempting to cover her body with her hands, she sent me back into the house for clothes. I remember how frustrated she was and that she sort of moaned and cried harder when I returned with only an apron. I was too little to even think about what she needed, and I was terrified that I'd be attacked. At the time, I didn't know that I was safe, that my father's rage was not directed, nor would it ever be directed, at me. I also didn't understand that the "White Lightning" and home brew my father made and drank were contributing factors.

It went on until my brother grew tall enough and strong enough to stop it. I remember the night it ended, with my brother standing over my father, whom he had just knocked to the living room floor. It was about 2 a.m. The incident drove a wedge between my brother and father that never healed. But the beatings finally stopped. Or at least I think they did.

My dreams about them didn't. Years after I was married, I would sit bolt upright in bed screaming as I recalled my mother's bloody face. She and I never talked about it until I moved back to Richmond and I finally got the nerve to broach the subject one afternoon. I didn't know until then that my mother, like so many abused women, had left and returned to my father several times, once when all four of us kids were under the age of 10. She had gone to her parents' home in Radford and was try-ing to find a job. With only a sixth-grade education, a factory position was all she could hope for. My grandmother and my uncle, a teenager at the time, were waiting in the car with one of my sisters while my mother went for the job interview. When she returned to the car, she discovered that my uncle had slapped my sister for misbehaving, leaving fin-gerprints on her face. My mother explained her return to my father—at least on that occasion—by saying, "Your Daddy never touched you children. He only hit me."

Some people will condemn me for writing this. They'll say, "You don't air family troubles." I might agree if I didn't feel at times like I'd grown up in World War III, if I didn't break out in a sweat when someone raises his voice or if I didn't have to steel myself not to run from any sort of altercation.

The time is ripe for speaking out. If not now, when? I think even my father would agree. At 88, he's mellowed and has lost that ugly edge, probably to a large degree because he stopped drinking. He is, by nature, a gentle man whom I've grown to love and respect. However, when his illiteracy was mixed with alcohol and the pressures of feeding four children, the recipe spelled disaster for somebody. That somebody was my mother.

If the women's liberation movement did anything, it gave women a voice—one that will no longer be silent. And, if I've learned nothing else from this year of research, I've learned that domestic violence and sexual assault are still so prevalent one might think they have been added to the water supply along with fluoride. It's not just pushing or shoving; it's vicious premeditated injury with life-threatening overtones, and it's pervasive in all strata of society. If it's to be confronted and, God willing, overcome, then it must be brought to light. I'm reminded of Hemingway's advice to other writers when he adjured them to write the truest sentence they knew how.

I have. ≋

October 2001

31

The Implosion of Our Lives
Finding solace away from home

I JUST HAD TO FIND A CHURCH. Something inside of me begged for reassurance, for the comfort that I always feel within a sanctuary. I left the hotel where I was attending a conference of the National Federation of Press Women and walked for what seemed like forever before discovering Christ Church Cathedral in downtown Indianapolis, Ind. I heard the tolling of the bell before I saw it.

The sound of the bell every few seconds was a mournful reminder of the days just past. This bell was tolling for all of America, especially for New York and its survivors as well as the nearly 3,000 lost, including some 300, maybe more, brave firefighters and police officers.

I didn't know if the church was open; I just hoped it was. Above the archway an American flag flapped gently in the warm breeze beside a banner that announced times for special services that day, Sept. 14, declared a national day of mourning by

President George W. Bush three days after the terrorist attacks at the Word Trade Center and Pentagon.

The sanctuary had only four people in it. I quietly stepped inside a pew midway of the church, knelt on the bench in front of me and allowed the silence to wrap its arms around me, feeling safe for the first time since the nightmare began. A large cream-colored candle burned in front of the sanctuary. The gigantic pipe organ was silent, but sunshine reflecting off the stained glass windows cast a kaleidoscope of muted rainbows onto the tall pipes.

Feeling renewed, I returned to the sunlight and noticed a big police officer sitting astride a motorcycle. He balanced the bike just beside the walkway, where the steps leading up to a nearby military memorial were strewn with red, white and blue balloons, burning candles and bouquets of flowers. The officer seemed lost in thought. I approached quietly and asked if I could talk with him. He nodded affirmatively. I introduced myself and asked, "Why are you here?"

"I have to stop every now and then," he said. "It's been a very rough week." Instinctively, I reached to hug him and he returned the favor. I knew it wasn't the first, nor would it be the last, embrace that someone, even perfect strangers, would bestow on him that week.

I returned for the last prayer service of the day — solemn, dignified and ecumenical. The priest in a flowing pale lavender robe extolled the attendees by saying, "We are Jews, Muslims and Christians searching for unity. The members of Islam are being blamed; it's senseless, wrong. We need prayers for unity, and I thank God you are here."

The overflowing crowd stood for the majority of the service, which included Scripture reading in English as well as Spanish. It was over much too quickly, the mind-numbing hurt too deep to be erased in 20 minutes. I stood in the sanctuary for a while, not wanting to leave the comfort zone. A lone usher approached and asked if I was all right. Suddenly I began to cry. I told him my older son has been a firefighter for 17 years in Fairfax County and my younger son might be called up with his Army reserve unit. He instinctively reached out and hugged me, just as I had hugged the officer, and asked where I was from. When I replied "Virginia," he laughed and said, "I went to Virginia Tech."

John Williams walked me to the front of the church where a lone teenage girl stood carefully counting off seconds before reaching above her head to pull on the large rope that created the doleful sound of the bell. The ringers had been taking turns all day, and the only time the bell had been silent was during the multiple prayer services. The teenager reminded me of our public servants, as well as our military, doing a job we don't always see and take for granted most of the time.

Somewhat at loose ends because the conference had allowed a free evening, I decided to attend a jazz fest at the Madame C.J. Walker Theatre Center. I entered the elevator with a man dressed in all black, with a gold crucifix hanging midway down his chest. He had an aura of serenity that was almost tangible. He turned out to be a retired pas-

pastor who loved playing piano.

He introduced me to Margaret Smith, assuring company for me before seating himself at the keyboard. Margaret, the sickle cell project director at the Martin Center in Indianapolis, turned out to be the master of ceremonies for the program. She slipped to the microphone later and welcomed me by name and press affiliation — Virginia Press Women. She even requested a special song for me.

Throughout the night, I was soothed by the skill of Marvin Chandler's fingers. I just knew those same hands had often played across pages of Scripture bringing comfort to his parishioners much the same way he was soothing the crowd that night with music.

The band stopped promptly at 7 p.m. to join other Americans who were pausing to light candles in a show of solidarity across the nation. Even the low murmuring ceased as we reflected on the tragedy. It seemed odd, but somehow appropriate, when the band started up again and Mary Moss stepped to the mike to begin a low crooning song, doing what others like her have always done, helping the rest of us by filling aching voids with music.

While the band rested, Marvin remembered a time almost exactly 30 years earlier when he was one of two ministers asked to help negotiate the Attica prison riot, which ultimately ended with 43 deaths.

"Evil," he said, "knows no race or nationality. People ask, 'Where is God? How do we see God in something like this?' I see Him in the love, compassion and courage that people have shown in spite of this terrible thing. It seems to me that I'm challenged even more by Jesus' words — words that defy any logic. He didn't give us a treatise or a lecture; he just said, 'Love your enemies.' It's a moral ambiguity. Martin Luther King Jr. did what he did in that way. If you love your enemy, that enemy brings judgment upon himself. They will have victory only if we become like them. My answer is to trust God and seek with everything in me to love my enemy."

I left Indianapolis the next morning under a beautiful sunny sky and headed for an airport that seemed to have more security personnel than travelers.

Back in Richmond, Va., I thought about the past week, where strangers had embraced me during a national tragedy, while I was so far from home. John Williams' words to me in the doorway of the church keep coming to mind. Noting Virginia's close proximity to Washington, he said, "You tell those folks in Virginia that they have people in Indiana who love them."

It's no wonder the Hoosier state is considered part of the heartland. ≋

November 2001

32

From a Henhouse to a Mansion
Executive chef took 'circuitous' career path

"IT ALL STARTED ON A LITTLE farm in rural Kentucky, milking goats, collecting eggs from the henhouse and digging potatoes for hours with my sister," Mark Herndon says. "We were young and worked hard, but we had fun. You couldn't go next door to see if Johnny could play. We were out in the country."

The path from a 40-acre farm in Murray, Ky., to Richmond, Va., took a circuitous route through Texas, New York and Williamsburg before Herndon became the youngest chef to be employed at Virginia's executive mansion beginning in 1995. He was 23; it was midway through George Allen's term as governor. Six years later and now serving Jim and Roxane Gilmore and their two teenage sons, Herndon walks through the mansion relating historical details as if he's always been there, being stumped only when he realizes some paintings have been changed, scrambling his tour details momentarily. He takes it in stride, like other changes in his busy day.

"We have to be extremely flexible. There are situations where dignitaries might be visiting and it has to go off flawlessly. Even when I have my schedule planned out, anything can happen."

Herndon explains the cadre of staff involved in meals served either in a breakfast nook where five guests can eat or in the state dining room, which can accommodate 60 guests for a luncheon or formal dinner.

"When an event comes up, Donna Case, the mansion director; her assistant, Amy Finch; the butler, Martin Townes and I look at the type of event, number of guests and whether it's a reception or dinner," Herndon says. "I plan the menu and wine selections accordingly. One full-time sous chef, Thomas Sears, and some part-time cooks also assist me. The more formal black-tie dinners, often six courses, are the most challenging because I have more to plan. We often rent tables, ballroom chairs, china, have menu cards printed."

Herndon says both the Allens and Gilmores prefer to keep dinner parties to around 30 guests. The dining room, including a table that seats 28, was added in 1906, when the kitchen was brought inside the mansion. That was the last time there was any significant remodeling.

Virginia's current First Lady chaired the executive committee for the recent mansion renovation, which took six months to complete, with crews working double shifts. Herndon was an integral member of that committee.

"I gave the architect my wish list for the kitchen," Herndon says, walking across the new gray, herringbone-pattern floor.

"I was so proud of the opportunity for staff input; we were taken very seriously. The kitchen was upgraded to that of restaurant quality, with a walk-in refrigerator and freezer, commercial equipment, gas, etc. Before, if I wanted to serve steaks, I was out the back door using the Weber grill, sometimes under an umbrella."

Herndon says significant changes have been made to the building, which was constructed in 1813, and is the oldest continuously occupied governor's mansion in the country. New bathroom facilities were added, along with a handicapped accessible elevator and the very first sprinkler system. The only real damage the mansion has seen was a fire on Jan. 4, 1926, when Governor Trinkle's son was playing with a sparkler and ignited the Christmas tree.

Christmas holidays pose yet another special chore for Herndon's staff.

The chef rolls his blue eyes and laughs about making 2,000 cookies for visitors to enjoy during the mansion's annual open house—a scenario Herndon couldn't have imagined when he began working as a 15-year-old in a Western Sizzlin' near Dallas. Herndon probably couldn't have imagined sleeping in a mansion either.

"A small bedroom is provided," he explains. "If I work late and we have a breakfast the next day, I don't go home."

Home for Herndon was Williamsburg, where he formerly worked as a rounds chef—a chef trained in all different areas—at the Williamsburg Inn. He learned of an opening at the mansion while attending a national chef's convention in New York. After being hired, he commuted from Williamsburg for four and a half years before relocating to the West End. He still travels but only across the river several times each week for a favorite pastime—working out at the Southside location of American Family Fitness.

"I had very little physical activity in my life and had added a few pounds from tasting every component of each meal," Herndon says. "Dave Johnson, a state trooper at the mansion, lives on the Southside and invited me to go to American Family with him. At first, I was intimidated. I saw fellows bench-pressing huge amounts and I'm lifting junior weights. But, I really grew to enjoy the staff and the special friends I've made there. I've lost about 25 pounds this past year, but I'd like to lose a little bit more," Herndon says as he pats his stomach. "But the holidays are coming."

A holiday for Herndon usually doesn't include a trip home to Dallas, where his parents still live.

"I've been here for six years and I've never had Thanksgiving off. I usually get Christmas Day, but it's not enough time to go home. My Mom makes the best turkey dressing," he says longingly.

In fact, Herndon hasn't gone home for Christmas since 1993, when he graduated from the Culinary Institute of America, the most prestigious culinary school in the country. Herndon eventually hopes to become a Certified Master Chef and have his own restaurant, which would probably require even more hours.

"It comes with the job," he says. "Even when you're not with family, you should put your heart into the food you're preparing — a little love. You don't always need a recipe with 35 ingredients. It can be something simple and very well done. The experience is created by the combination of food, the setting and the people you share it with." ≋

December 2001

33

Orphan Feet and Ice Cream Treats
Shoe drive offers sweet reward

IT'S JANUARY, but I'm still thinking about summertime, sandals and ice cream. I'd never eaten Häagen-Dazs ice cream until last August, and then it was a gift. Sort of. It all started with an e-mail message that reads:

> *Subject: Shoes for Orphan Souls*
> *Dear Family and Friends: Mark and I thought we would spread the news about this very worthwhile charity drive. We really know firsthand how much these orphan children need shoes. When we were in Kazakhstan to get Alia we saw that all the shoes on the children's feet were old and ill-fitting, certainly something you would not want to put on YOUR kids' feet. The list below has information about where drop-off areas will be located in mall areas around the nation.*

The message, from Julie Grimes and her husband, Mark Fagerburg, said the Richmond drop-off point was the Chesterfield Towne Center.

I'd known Julie professionally for years, but when she was diagnosed with breast cancer in 1997, we formed a bond that will last a lifetime. She and Mark surprised me when they let me tag along for doctor visits, surgeries and reconstruction so I could write about their experience and how Julie was cancer free after surgery, not needing radiation or chemotherapy. Shortly thereafter, they surprised me again when they announced their decision to adopt after 15 years of marriage without children.

Nine months after their adoption application was filed, Mark and Julie returned from a whirlwind trip to Kazakhstan with Alia, a 3-year-old ball of fire with beautiful almond-shaped eyes, shiny brown hair and enough inquisitiveness to exhaust the world. Thus, their slam-dunk introduction into the world of children's shoes.

I kept thinking of little toes as I rummaged through my closet looking for something appropriate to donate. The collected shoes were going to children between birth and 18. I settled on a pair of sling-back, open-toed sassy beige pumps from the closet shelf. They were brand new, but I thought, "What the heck; it's for a good cause and I've got more shoes than feet, so...."

Shoes in hand, I approached the information desk at Chesterfield Towne Center. I was told, "The collection point is just beyond that Häagen-Dazs kiosk." I walked through the crowd and found the booth where I learned that only new shoes were accepted, because of customs regulations.

I also learned that Noelynn Koo, marketing direct or for Macerich Company, which owns the Towne Center, and Melissa Lynch, manager of the Disney store located in the mall, were volunteering their time. They'd been sitting beneath the boiling skylights for two weekends during the record-breaking heat in August. Undaunted, Noelynn grinned and said, "Well, it was the most visible place in the mall, so here we are. In the last two weekends, we've collected 300 pairs of shoes."

I learned that KCBI Radio in Dallas/Fort Worth had started the shoe drive, originally called Shoes for Russian Souls, in 1995. Together they collected more than 5,000 pairs of new shoes between 1995 and 1998. In 1999, Buckner Orphan Care International assumed the leadership role, while Children's Hope Chest continued to help with the distribution in Russia. The 2000 drive collected more than 50,000 pairs. Various trucking firms donated transportation of the shoes to Dallas for distribution and sorting before they were delivered to children in Russia, Romania, China, Mexico, Africa, Latvia, Croatia, Ukraine, Belarus and India, as well as the United States.

After chatting a few minutes, Noelynn said, "I'm going to give you a receipt. You can take it to the Häagen-Dazs kiosk for free ice cream."

Keith Bennett, manager of the station who came up with the idea to give away the ice cream as a bonus to donators, suggested Dulce de Leche (caramel), a good recommendation it turned out.

"We wanted to be involved and couldn't print fliers or anything, so I thought this might be a little extra reward," Keith said.

I wandered through the mall enjoying the unexpected treat. Suddenly the shoes that every child was wearing became important. There were tennis shoes, wedgies, stilted heels, sandals, beat up brogues and paint-dripped canvas shoes. The most memorable was a lime green pair of jelly flip-flops with metallic stars embedded in the soles. They were held on to a teenage girl's foot by only a big toe loop. I stood there for about 20 minutes and never saw a child without shoes, except two little towheads in strollers. I couldn't help but think of what Julie had told me about Alia when they were shopping for shoes to donate.

"I explained that we were getting shoes to give to the children at orphanages like the one where she lived, "Julie said. "Alia asked, 'Are we getting on an airplane and flying to Kazakhstan to give the shoes to the children?'

"Alia was satisfied that we just had to take them to the mall," Julie added. "When we got there, she marched right up with the shoes and told the volunteers that she was from Kazakhstan and didn't have nice shoes when she lived there before she had a Mommy and a Daddy. They gave Alia a wonderful T-shirt that swallowed her whole; they had only one size. She insisted on putting it on and proudly wore it the rest of the day. Hopefully it encouraged others to make a donation."

You might not get ice cream, but you'd experience the same wonderful sense of delicious satisfaction, just like you'd eaten Häagen-Dazs, sans calories. ≋

January 2002

34

Bragging Rights Begin
Grandmother-to-be goes into training

Mɪ Y LATE HUSBAND always said if I ever were arrested, it would be for playing with babies' toes. I just can't help it. I'd walk a mile to touch one of those little pink nubbins. Did you know the best place for finding little feet sans socks and shoes is during the summer in long grocery store lines?

Even though I've always been gaga about babies, I've never had much interest in becoming a grandmother. Didn't have a thing to do with age; I just truly wasn't very interested, even though my two sons have asked on occasion if I'd enjoy having a grandchild. The question came up again Saturday, Jan. 12.

"Hi Mom," my older son, Beau, said when he called. He calls often, so I didn't think anything was amiss, until he said, "Leila is on the phone too."

"Well, that's unusual," I replied.

"That's because this is an unusual phone call," he said.

"We're pregnant!" Leila fairly squealed.

Lucky for me, I was sitting on the bed. I promptly fell backward and began to whoop. Do you think this is a harbinger of things to come?

Since I didn't have any experience in the field, I decided I needed help. After all, my first reaction was to ask my son a week later, "What's the first cuss word I can teach the kid?" and "How old does it have to be before it can jump out of an airplane with me?"

I need to insert here that my sweet red-haired daughter-in-law is of a more genteel nature than her Brillo-haired mother-in-law. She abides me very well and understands that I gave her the Sweet Baboo of her life—who made this grandchild possible, I might add.

I decided to poll some of my friends on the subject. I called Gay Neale, a fellow writer and dear friend in Brunswick County, Va. Gay, 66, became a grandmother in 2000.

I posed the question in an e-mail: What's different about being a grandmother?

Her response: "I'm a calm, collected, mature person, not given to huge displays of emotion or excitement. I have looked in the past with thinly disguised disdain at people who flip out pictures and talk about 'cute' and 'adorable' grandprogeny. Heaven help me, I thought, I'd never be like that.

"After my grandson was born, I found I had a tattered bunch of photos in my wallet and was using words like, 'amazing, smart, adorable.'

"The cruncher was when I accompanied my

daughter to a 1-year-old's birthday party, aswarm with little ones and their mothers. I found myself feeling a kindly pity for every other mother there; their little one was not nearly so beautiful or active or interesting as Aiden! I made the mistake of saying this to my daughter. Now it's a family story."

Gay also said, "Grandmothering brings out things in you that you never knew you had, like sweater knitting, incredible tolerance and patience ('Once upon a time there were three little bunnies...' for the 100th time.) But it also brings out a love you never knew you were capable of."

For a second opinion, I posed the same question to Diane Dillard, a Richmond friend.

Diane, who became a grandmother at 48, said, "I seemed to have gone through my son and daughter's growing-up years in a daze. I was so busy surviving that I missed a lot. My two grandsons have given me an opportunity to relive my children's early years. My daughter made a special box of 'firsts' for each of them. I would never have thought of doing that. It's wonderful to see things through my grandchildren's eyes. They are so fresh and innocent."

While all of that information was encouraging, one question Beau and Leila asked me on the day they sprung the news kept bugging me.

"What do you want to be called?" each of them asked in turn.

I want to go on record right now as disliking "Granny," "Grandma", and "Gammy." None of those ordinary names for me. I want something unusual. A typical writer, I turned to research for answers. Also typically, I called the wonderful folks who work at the Bon Air Library.

Within a few minutes I had more names for grandmother than I would ever need. Here are just a few, as well as their origins, the librarian dug up for me:

> *Grand'mere – French*
> *Nonna – Italian*
> *Abuela – Spanish*
> *Bedstemoder – Danish*
> *Mormor/Farmor – maternal/paternal*
>   *grandmother – Swedish*
> *Ovo' – Portuguese*
> *Anneanne/Babaanne – maternal/paternal*
>   *grandmother – Turkish*

I pondered these and also considered Bubbe, my personal favorite, which is Yiddish. Then the magic moniker rolled up. The librarian discovered that Polish kids call their grandmothers Babka. Now I was cooking, since my younger son, Jason, has an "intended" of Polish descent.

I called Jason's Monika and enlisted her help. Babka (pronounced Bobka), she explained was the "formal" way of saying grandmother. She then said that "special" grandmothers were referred to as "Babcia," (pronounced Bobcheea), which has a soothing, gentle sound. That settled it. Not only would I be "special," I'd ensure the grandkids-to-come that they needn't fret over pronunciation. Until the wee ones can say it, they can shorten it to Bubbe, my second best choice.

That decision made, the only thing left for me to do was to begin practicing my favorite nursery jingle, the one I always used when I bathed my boys and kissed their little toes one at a time.

> *This little piggy went to market.*
> *This little piggy stayed home.*
> *This little piggy had ham.*
> *This little piggy had none.*
> *This little piggy cried "Wee, wee, wee," all the*
> *way home.*

Come on September. ≋

April 2002

35

A Mother's Day Portrait
Stove-side chats mixed food with advice

Mʏ ᴍᴀᴍᴀ lived to feed others. It was always a defining moment when she managed to get something into another person's mouth, especially her children or grandchildren. One of her favorite duties was preparing fudge for the grandchildren at Christmas. To my delight, I was in her kitchen the last time she made it.

"Open that can of Carnation milk and pour it over the sugar in the black frying pan," she said to me. "Now, stir it up good until it's completely melted. When you move it to the stove, be sure you put that burner on No. 3—the fudge will cook too fast if it's any higher. Now, you watch it, and don't stir it too much. It'll take about 10 minutes to boil."

Mama stood bent almost perpendicular to the stove. She leaned on one arm, lost in her chore of making the first of the usual two batches of fudge. Intent on her job, she was unaware that I was studying her so closely. I wanted to remember that day. I wondered, as I often did, how many more times I'd have the privilege of being at her elbow while she cooked.

What she was wearing became stamped in my memory—an orange blouse with a scooped-out neck. It had little daisies with teal centers surrounded by tiny green leaves. Over the blouse, she wore a pale green sweater. Over that sweater, she wore another beige one with cable-knit stitches going up each arm from her wrist to her shoulder. Her slacks were bright red, matching tiny red stripes that were part of a U.S. flag—the stitched adornment on top of her navy blue slip-on bedroom shoes—a gift from her sister, Geneva, during a recent visit. Just as I was inwardly smiling at the plethora of colors, she said, "I need to rest now and catch my breath." She sat down on her black kitchen stool opposite the stove—removed from the work but still close enough to give orders.

Taking over the watchman position for the fudge, I, too, finally relaxed. I had been holding my breath for fear the hot syrup would pop out and scorch her frail and shaky hand. I watched as she struggled to take in air, the ever-present oxygen tube running from her nostrils, draped around each ear and secured in place beneath her chin. The skin on her neck hung in folds and her hair, completely white, was a little askew. Then 81, I couldn't help but think of how she used to look, with dark chestnut wavy hair, smooth clear skin and laughing, sharp brown eyes. When I was a child, those eyes could send a message without her saying a word. One look meant I'd better be quiet. A second one steeled me in place for fear of the ever-present threat of having to go and fetch my own willow switch. Although I had lots of practice at finding switches, I never found one that didn't leave a welt on tender legs. I still marvel at the fact that the weeping willow is my favorite tree.

Another favorite of mine is October beans, a specialty my daddy grew year after year in his garden. I used to hate shelling them in the summer, when I was a child. My parents, my brother and two sisters and I would gather in the late afternoon on the front porch of the little white farmhouse where we lived in Christiansburg, Va. We'd all sit on the porch, dip into the huge stainless steel tub and retrieve big handfuls of Octobers to fill the pans resting on our laps. I can still remember sore thumbs from cracking open the milky yellow pod to reveal the bulbous beans covered with deep cranberry stripes, signifying the bean was ripe.

I relive those times often now. They have taken on more significance recently. My mother died February 23, 2001. Shortly after her death, I decided I should cook some of her canned October beans. They were always comforting, when steeped to perfection in a soupy brown broth and accompanied by my mama's special coleslaw. Though she gave me directions on how to make it before she died, I've still got a ways to go. Even Mama's siblings used to say, "Can't anybody make coleslaw like Beulah Mae."

As Mother's Day approaches, memories of her wash over me. While I was sorting some of her things, I came across a Mother's Day gift that I gave to her years ago. It's two picture frames, one bearing a print of Renoir's "On the Terrace," first painted in 1881. It depicts a woman sitting in a garden with a little girl at her elbow. The child has her hand on a bowl of fruit, as if expecting to share it with her maternal friend. The other frame holds a poem by Thomas W. Fessenden, who must have had a mother like mine. It's titled "A Portrait of My Mother" and reads:

You painted no madonnas
On chapel wall in Rome,
But with a diviner touch
Upon the walls of home.

You wrote no lofty poems
With rare poetic art;
But with a finer vision
You put poems in my heart.

You carved no shapeless marble
To symmetry divine;
But with a nobler genius
You shaped this soul of mine.

You built no great cathedrals
The centuries applaud
But with a grace exquisite
Your heart was house of God.

Had I the gift of Raphael
Or Michelangelo,
Oh, what a rare Madonna
My mother's life would show. ≋

May 2002

36

When Father Doesn't Know Best
An aging parent floats away from reality

THE HOSPITAL ATTENDANT peered at my sister and me from behind my father's head.

"We'll be moving very fast," she said. "You'll have to keep up."

She tilted my father's wheelchair back on two wheels and left the emergency room with me in close pursuit.

Following a quick ride in an elevator and entrance through an electronically locked door, we bypassed a plethora of patients heading straight for 362B East, Tucker's Pavilion—the third floor, which houses geriatric psychiatric patients. My 88-year-old father would spend the next eight days and nights there.

I felt as if I had just descended into hell and there was no exit. We had arrived at Chippenham Hospital at 4:30 a.m. Six hours later, I realized it was Sunday, Feb. 17. Suzanne Lee was the "charge" nurse on duty at Tucker's that day. She followed us quickly into the room, introduced herself and then turned her full attention to my befuddled father.

With expertise that comes from longtime

practice, she deftly unwrapped my father's frail body from beneath the wide bands that ensured he didn't leap from his wheelchair.

"Come on, sweetie, let's dance," she said very quietly, sliding her hands just inside my father's arms.

For the first time since our arrival, a look of complete trust came over my father. He allowed Suzanne to gently lift and waddle him over to the bed. I'm sure he felt the struggle was over, when it was just beginning.

My father's descent into dementia began much earlier than any of our family members realized. There were subtle signs—confusion over what day it was, sleeping during the day, staying up at night and increased anger. We didn't recognize anger as part of dementia because my father had naturally stayed angry about something all of his life, whether it was a loud child or a stray hog getting out of a pen. A completely irascible person, he never seemed happy unless he was in the midst of some brouhaha. My siblings and I soon learned that what we perceived as normal contention was just a primer of things to come.

Time became a blur as my two sisters, Janet and Doris, and I struggled to maintain a vigil for my father, who was vacillating wildly between almost complete mania and comatose stupor from medication. There didn't seem to be a middle ground. Whenever he was conscious enough to realize he wasn't at home, he became combative and uncivil. So round and round we went with different medications as the psychiatrist tried to find the magic combination of drugs necessary to calm my father's—and our—tattered nerves.

There were times when we couldn't decide whether to laugh or cry, so we took turns doing both. Some of the things Daddy said were both awful and hysterical, like when he told one of the nurses, "You're a pretty black woman, but you're too big," or when he said to my brother, "Harless, I'm glad you brought me a toothpick. I needed to get some of this tough mule meat out of my teeth."

The experience was so surreal that there were days when I felt like I was in a scene from *One Flew Over the Cuckoo's Nest*, except for Tucker's lack of restraints and its kindness—inordinate kindness, the sort you notice after hours of observation. It's the hand that's offered to steady a patient who needs anchoring. It's the gentle word and tone of voice used when a patient is terribly confused and wants to go home. It's the quiet directive to a patient who has wandered into an unassigned room or has begun to disrobe in the day area.

Some days, my father's roommate seemed to stay out of his clothes more than he stayed in them. I noticed "Mr. A" standing in the halls sans clothes one morning. I was about to alert Suzanne, when she came through the door, spotted the naked gentleman and calmly said, "Oh, this is not good." Without a flinch, she gently guided him back into his room and helped him re-dress.

I witnessed that scene, and others just as bizarre, many, many times. The week that followed seemed like a year. I saw the shifts change with the perfunctory "reporting" of what happened on the previous watch; I studied the various staff member's personalities, wondering how they could be so patient during a single, much less a double, shift. I noted the different sizes, shapes, colors and nationalities of the doctors, nurses, aides, occupational therapists and social workers. I saw the patients get familiar enough with each other to tell when one had improved or worsened. I saw the lady whom I had dubbed "Wander Woman" drift in and out of rooms, once emerging with white bubbles all over her face and hair.

A surprised nurse quickly dipped her finger into the white stuff, smelled it and proclaimed, "Shaving cream." No scolding was heard then, or ever, because "Wander Woman" was everyone's surrogate grandmother at Tucker's. Without saying a word, she gently began patting my shoulder the night we arrived, somehow knowing that I needed comfort and that she was providing it. She was part of the living drama being played out in each person's life, whether it was a patient, family or staff member in that cloistered, make-believe world.

I began to see the patients as liquid in a lava lamp. Some were practically stationary, but others would pop up at any time and float around. Since Janet and I didn't know their names, we made some up for them. "New York" was the tall, intelligent gentleman who carried a copy of *The New York Times* around in a grocery bag. He consistently told us that he was a "member in good standing" at Tucker's. "Tattoo" had arms heavily adorned with black-and-red scenes. He smiled often at my father and one day actually embraced him and said, "Hey, Pop Pop, looks like you're feeling better today."

Some days the "sitters" became "floaters" in the daily dance, with partners occasionally cutting in on each other. The staff continued bathing and feeding patients, changing beds and diapers, tenderly dressing wounds and dispensing medicine with a routine that was almost musically orchestrated. In the morning and afternoon, there was a flurry of physicians. Some stayed briefly. Others lingered, patiently answering questions that were probably all the same, just voiced through different mouths.

On my father's last day at Tucker's, he was doing a jig with his walker and inviting other patients to sing "Cripple Creek" with him. The day before that, two employees from Southerland Place, a nursing home in Midlothian, had come to visit and had asked Daddy if he wanted to go with them out to a nice place in the country.

That night, he announced, "Two girls was here today wanting me to help on a farm. I told 'em I'd do it. They was so young, I knowed they couldn't manage by theirselves." ≋

July 2002

37

A Silent Message

In the face of loss, strength sometimes comes from unexpected places

Dr. Linda Tiffany, the owner of the Women's Counseling Center in Richmond, has often said to me, "One loss represents all losses." Linda explained this to me after my husband died suddenly in September 1991. She has repeated it to me several times as I have dealt with other losses, the most significant one being my mother's death in February 2001.

The death of a loved one is an unusually singular event, and while it's catastrophic to the family and individuals it affects, it goes primarily unnoticed by most people. I have never felt so alone as I did in the first two years directly following my husband's death. The only place I could find real solace was at the ocean near the Nags Head Fishing Pier in North Carolina, where our family always vacationed. That's where my older son, Beau, and I left my husband's ashes at dawn, to be taken out with the tide, along with three long-stemmed red roses, a few weeks after my husband's untimely death at the age of 49. The roses symbolized the remaining family members. My younger son, Jason, elected to take a portion of his father's ashes and have his own private ceremony in Myrtle Beach, SC, near his Coastal Carolina University campus.

I had planned a quiet walk along that beach on my way to visit Jason in March 1994. Although the temperature was moderate, the wind still wrapped a chill around my neck, and a cup of hot coffee was just what I needed. Along with the coffee, I got an unexpected bonus when I stopped at the Second Avenue Pier.

There I met a middle-aged man with a neatly trimmed white beard. He wore a pale blue shirt, black jeans, a leather belt and wire-rimmed glasses. I remember his piercing eyes. I think they were blue. Regardless of the color, their gaze was so direct and so defiant, I felt as if a splash of brilliant light had just danced across my vision.

The man nodded as I said, "Good morning."

I ordered coffee and he turned sideways to pour it, revealing a thick scar that cut deeply across his throat, leaving its jagged signature from his ear down toward his chin.

"Anything biting?" I asked.

He shook his head from side to side.

"What about the charter boats?"

With a quick movement of his hand, he grabbed a child's blackboard slate from the counter, picked up a piece of chalk, scribbled a few words, punched a period at the end and turned the slate for me to read.

"I understand the boats going out 15 to 20 miles are doing good."

After I acknowledged that I'd read it, he roughly swiped the slate clean, placed it back on the counter and looked away. I thanked him, took my coffee and walked toward the beach, but I didn't get very far. I had to sit down to contemplate what had just transpired.

I was suddenly overcome with compassion for that stranger, whose name I didn't even know. I wondered how he faced each day. He speaks, yet he doesn't make a sound. I thought of him and the enormous courage he'd have to muster each morning, knowing that he will be vulnerable every time a customer walks into the pier store. My coffee got cold as tears made pockmarks in the sand between my feet.

I wondered how the man would beckon a dog, answer a phone, whisper "I love you." How would he warn a child of impending danger, call for an ambulance, describe how he feels or express himself at the height of lovemaking? So many questions that I couldn't ask him and he couldn't answer. Probably only the ocean knows his secrets.

I also wondered if he had any idea of his effect on me. Without saying a word, he had spoken to me just by being there, by facing the cruel limitations life had forced on him. I wondered how I could tell him I admired him. I finally decided I would use his medium.

I wrote a note and walked slowly back to the pier. Still standing behind the counter, he looked up, then held out his hand. He was offering to refill my coffee. I handed him my cup then laid the note where he could see it when he turned back to me.

"Sir: I don't know you, but today I heard you

speak. You have spoken to me of trials and tough times and overcoming pain. I have to tell you that without a word you have given me a message I needed to hear. My husband's ashes are in this ocean, and yet he speaks to me from his strength, just as you have. I am a writer and I will write about seeing you some day. If you would like a copy of the article, please leave your name and address on this notepad. I'll be in touch with you. It may be a while before this publishes. I'm a fairly new freelance writer. Thank you."

He looked at me more gently this time, with an almost discernible smile, and picked up the pen to write his name and address. I filed the notepad away but I never forgot about the man or the incident. I rediscovered my notes again recently.

I'm going to send a copy of this to Bob Ginevan. I know he still lives in Myrtle Beach, but he has an unlisted phone number, so I'm going to use his medium of communication again. I'm going to tell him that although it has taken me almost eight years to let him know it, I regularly count him among my blessings, and that ironically I'm writing this on what would have been my 38th wedding anniversary. I want to tell him that I'm sorry for his struggles but I'm so thankful I had an opportunity to witness his particular brand of courage. He was not only a symbol of hope for me when I needed it desperately but was the personification of a saying I've often heard.

When God closes a door, he always opens a window. ≋

November 2002

38

The Urge to Purge
A new year brings the desire to get rid of clutter–in all its forms

"'Begin at the beginning,' said the King gravely, 'and go till you come to the end, then stop.'"
– The King of Hearts, *Alice in Wonderland*

F OR ONCE IN MY LIFE, I AM A perfect 10. I knew I was home free when I answered "yes" to each of the following questions, which were asked during a meeting held at the Koger Center Holiday Inn a few months back.

1) *Do things often get lost in your house?*
2) *Do you ever buy something you already have at home but don't want to look for?*
3) *Do you have things collecting on top of your microwave, kitchen table, piano or refrigerator?*
4) *Do you ever drop something and say you're putting it there "for now"?*
5) *Do you have stacks of magazines or newspapers saved for that day when you can clip the stories, coupons or recipes?*

6) *Do you have large files of things to be filed?*
7) *Do you spend a lot of your waking hours wondering what you'll have for dinner?*
8) *Do you make lists, forget where you parked your car or which car you drove?*
9) *Do you save things you cannot use, like brown bags filled with brown bags?*
10) *Do you frequently say, "I'll keep it because it might come in handy some day"?*

By the time Deniece Schofield—a professional organizer from Cedar Rapids, Iowa, who was in town to help disarrayed schmucks like me—asked the last question, I was wondering how I could slide under my chair without being noticed. When I got the courage to look around the room, I saw about 30 other women and one solitary man looking as guilty as I did. I stayed for the entire two-hour seminar on how to find order, something that only drifts through my life upon rare occasions, usually as writing deadlines approach.

Sometime last October I got another nudge from one of Jann Malone's columns in the *Richmond Times-Dispatch*, in which she wrote about upcoming "how-to" organizational meetings sponsored by the local Goodwill Industries' stores. The meetings were free, a surefire draw for me, and the object, I assume, was to swell the coffers of Goodwill, something I could do with very little assistance.

There were four sessions, which included tips

on how to divest oneself of all clutter, from home to office. I had planned on attending three of them but only managed to make two after I misplaced Jann's column and "thought" I remembered the times. When I got to the third meeting, it was just breaking up. So much for organization.

I did learn several things from Marie Bowling of Brooke, Va., the owner of Prescription for Order, a professional organizing service. I was especially inspired when she gave out chocolate candy for correct answers. She inspired me again by drawing my name out of a pot and giving me a book entitled *Let Go of Clutter*.

On the other hand, as soon as Marie was finished with her presentation, I promptly bought a cookie jar. Who could resist a duck dressed in one of those yellow slickers little kids used to wear to school when it was raining? I justified it by saying I'd make cookies, fill it up for a friend and deliver it on a rainy day.

At the other meeting, I learned from Debbie Bowie, a feng shui guru from Richmond, Va., that all things have energy. Seems clutter gives off bad energy and should be eliminated. Now that was real knowledge. While I couldn't get rid of the enormous piles of papers in my office, I could at least cover them, thereby stifling that clutter somewhat. I stuffed two huge boxes with papers and draped them with yellow towels, to match the duck, of course, which had found a new home in my office.

While I might make and deliver cookies, I have a feeling the "quacker" has found a permanent home. With my office a bit straighter, the duck looked a little out of place, so I went looking for another cookie jar to keep it company. I remembered a cookie jar my mother gave me years ago, her very first acquisition as a new bride, purchased with money she saved by selling eggs.

Mama's cookie jar is made like a Scottie dog, only white, and for some strange reason the dog has a blue scarf tied around its chin that ends in a bow right between its ears. Maybe it had a toothache. Anyway, the blue scarf matches the blue in the border of the room, which also has some yellow in it, which makes the duck feel right at home.

All this cleaning inspired me to come up with another list for which I again qualify as a perfect 10. I've decided to make and follow my own rules in 2003, which include pushing, pulling and purging everything that can be eliminated from my life. Here's the list. Some of it actually pertains to organization.

1) *I'll divest my life of all things that aren't beautiful. Color, I have learned over the last few years, is of paramount importance to my life. (See duck story above.)*
2) *If something isn't useful, I'll chuck it — regardless of whether it's clothing, food or furniture. The only sacred items are books, which defy all rules.*
3) *I'll resist buying reduced-price meat and keeping it in the freezer, "just in case" the kids need it.*
4) *I'll give away large, bulky items, like my 15-cubic-foot freezer. The kids didn't even notice it was gone.*

5) *I plan to permanently eliminate people from my life who take more energy than they add during a conversation or visit.*

6) *I'll keep nothing I can live without–some family members come to mind.*

7) *I'll not feel guilty about eating handfuls of chocolate. I've learned that, just like a kid, I'll get sick of it, which should act as a deterrent from similar behavior. Notice, I used the word should.*

8) *I'll attend only a single yard sale each month and limit purchases to what can be carried away in two hands.*

9) *I'll keep a box for giveaways by the front door and drop the things purchased at yard sales directly into the box. When it's full, I'll leave the box at the closest charity donation site.*

10) *Absolutely under no circumstances will I go back the next day, as I have done, and re-buy the same items.* ≋

January 2003

39

Life Lesson Finally Learned
Keeping it together can sometimes make a mess of things

Have you ever experienced a screamer—a moment that just left you walking the floor and asking yourself, "What were you thinking?"

My latest "screamer" happened on Nov. 9, 2002, the night my husband was posthumously inducted into the Chowan College Sports Hall of Fame in Murfreesboro, N.C. It was a beautiful fall day, with painted leaves gently falling on the 1848 campus, just as they did on the Saturdays when I used to cheer Oscar on at the school's football stadium. Known then as "Bear," Oscar was part of the 1963-64 team that came within one game of making it to Pasadena, Calif., to play in the Junior College Rose Bowl.

The Braves were a band of brothers who resembled a Bradley tank when walking shoulder to shoulder across campus. That team melded like no other, according to their coach, Jim Garrison, who was recently inducted into the North Carolina Sports Hall of Fame.

Oscar's upcoming honor sent me digging

through boxes looking for our 1964 annual, in which Oscar was pictured in a full-page photo with a caption that reads, "The Will to Win." That photo was a tribute to Oscar's determination to continue playing football after being diagnosed with severe juvenile diabetes. I wanted that photo for the ceremonial plaque. But, back to Garrison.

The coach planned to offer a tribute about Oscar. I sent him some remarks that my older son, Beau, had made at Oscar's memorial service, so Garrison could use them as a reference for Oscar's adult years. Much to my surprise, Garrison still had in his possession, 11 years after the fact, a tribute that my younger son, Jason, had written after his father's death. When it was published in the newspaper at Jason's school, Coastal Carolina University, I clipped it and sent it to Garrison, knowing he would deeply appreciate the comments Jason had made about Oscar and Chowan.

My part in the ceremony was to accept the plaque and say something meaningful. That's where the rub came in. Beau had strenuously objected to attending the ceremony, because he didn't want to see me cry nor be reminded of our loss. Prodded by his brother and me, Beau finally acquiesced and even offered to speak in my place.

Garrison called to tie up loose ends. When I said Beau would be accepting the plaque, in his Southern drawl Garrison stated, "If I had my druthers, I'd druther you do it." We both laughed, understanding he could still get what he wanted from his players.

At that point, I'd been crying intermittently for about three weeks. It started when Dave Witten, another inductee who played on the same team with Oscar, called to tell me of the honor. I also cried with Luddy Romano, another teammate and Oscar's closest friend at college, who later served as the best man in our wedding. Finally, Luddy started laughing and telling me stories, including one about accompanying Oscar and other team-mates to a burlesque show in a nearby town where a player had pulled a pin on the tent, closing down the event. The next day, police were swarming all over campus. Oscar had explained their presence to me with a tale about the players borrowing an elephant from a circus the night before and taking it for a stroll. Either way, Garrison made them run an indeterminable number of laps after the police left.

In a subsequent conversation, I asked Luddy if Oscar was nicknamed "Bear" because he had so much chest hair. I thought Luddy was going to choke with laughter. He finally said, "No way. It was because he was mean as cats — t on the football field."

The closer the time came for me to speak, the more panic I felt. After Garrison read from my sons' tributes to their father and then added a poem titled "The Winner," everyone was crying. The onus was on me, the last speaker.

It was the first time my sons had seen me speak in public, and I was determined to be strong. I repeated the stories I've just written, stories I ordi-narily wouldn't have shared with any audience, tame though they may seem by today's standards. Doing so enabled me to keep it together, but it also kept me from saying what needed to be said.

I would have cried if I'd described the lack of support Oscar had at home or how he took the sheets off his bed, put them in a grocery sack and thumbed a ride to Chowan for football tryouts his freshman year.

I couldn't say how he cried after opening a letter from his grandmother containing a $60 money order to finish paying for his college ring. Oscar worked flipping hamburgers when he wasn't in class or at practice, but he didn't have enough for the ring, and his parents wouldn't provide it for him, the first person in his family to attend college.

I couldn't explain how the ring, a prized possession, was accidentally thrown away by either Jason or his roommate in a cleaning frenzy one day. I had given the ring to Jason because he knew its significance and because he didn't have a chance to say goodbye to his father. I couldn't voice how Ralph Thurston, another teammate, and his wife, Mary, had paid for Oscar's Hall of Fame ring so Jason would have a replacement.

I couldn't describe the many times, as the horror of diabetes ate away at our lives, that we applied the lessons we'd learned by attending compulsory chapel three times a week at Chowan, that our faith was the cornerstone for our lives. I couldn't speak about Garrison becoming a surrogate father to his players, an example Oscar passed on to our sons.

After everyone left that night, I replayed the events in my mind. Suddenly, about 1 a.m., I realized what I had and had not said and knew that I could never rectify the situation.

In my determination not to cry, I hadn't listened

to my heart. I hadn't given nearly enough credit to Oscar for surpassing the devastating personal obstacles he had overcome to be part of that close-knit team. Instead, I told stories that would've been better left untold that night, although I did get a laugh when I related how Oscar had sent a Miller High Life up to my room in a brown bag by my room mother, who had to climb three flights of stairs to deliver it to me, a teetotaler. Had she opened the bag, we would've been excommunicated from that Baptist college within 24 hours, regardless of the fact that I had never even tasted beer in my life.

While that's hard to believe, I was only 17 then. I'm 57 now and I think I've finally learned that the price is too high for deviating from that quiet inner voice, the one that keeps us from repeating mistakes. Oscar's grandmother used to say, "A burned child is scared of fire."

I believe I'm well done. ≋

March 2003

40

A Friend In Deed
We all need somebody to lean on
in times of trouble

"What brings joy to the heart is not so much the friend's gift as the friend's love."

–St. Aelred of Rievaulx, *Christian Friendship*

I CALL HER "DR. DI, " BUT HER REAL NAME IS DIANE Dillard. I started calling her Dr. Di after I discovered her down-to-earth wisdom equaled—and sometimes surpassed—that of Dr. Phil, the famous psychologist, author and talk-show host.

Diane and I go way back. In fact, we lived next-door to each other in Chesterfield County for several years when we were teenagers. We both attended Manchester High School, where our mothers worked together in the cafeteria. After Diane married and I left for college, our paths didn't cross again for about 40 years.

That all changed the day Diane picked up a *Richmond Magazine* in a local doctor's office. She called Susan Winiecki, *Richmond*'s editor, and inquired as to whether the Nancy Wright Beasley who penned the article she had read might be the same Nancy Wright who grew up on Ruthers Road. Not knowing for sure, Susan faxed a story I had written about my father to Diane. When I got home that day, a distantly familiar voice on my answering machine was saying, "Hello, Nancy. This is Diane Lowry Dillard. Please call me."

I soon discovered that, without knowing it, I had been living within a half-mile of Diane for about eight years since relocating to Richmond. In the ensuing two years, Diane has become the personification of friendship. We even managed to reunite our mothers, who hadn't seen each other for over 20 years. Diane brought Mrs. Lowry to see my mother just three weeks before my mother died.

I leaned on Diane unreservedly when my precious mother died in February 2001, and I leaned again when my feisty father died in March. Diane's ever-present encouragement, notwithstanding the food, flowers, cards and books she has showered me with, has been nothing short of remarkable. Throughout any ordeal I've weathered, Diane's double-dimpled smile and hearty laugh have become mainstays for me. I have never — and I do mean never — called her when she hasn't offered a word of encouragement.

I thought I was through leaning on her so hard until the day my parents' home was sold. I went over to leave my key inside the house for the young man who would become the new owner the next day. When I went into my mother's kitchen for the last time, I saw that extra-wide stove (the one with enough room between the burners to flour oysters for frying) and then I glanced at the double-door refrigerator-freezer combination in matching avocado green. When I thought about all the family meals that had been cooked and served in that room, I came unglued. Suddenly I could see my father on all fours at Christmastime giving my two boys a piggyback ride and recall Mama's face as she read to my little niece, Wendy, used to get off the school bus at my parents' house and spend afternoons with Mama.

I looked around the room a final time, laid the key on the counter, picked up my Mama's beige dustpan and floor mop, pulled the kitchen door closed behind me and made a beeline for Diane's house. She welcomed me with open arms as usual and said, "What am I going to do with you?" She did what she always does: She hugged me, shored me up with a pep talk and sent me on my way with a handful of tissues. By the time I had gotten to the stop sign just beside her house, I felt infinitely better. Of course, Diane called me the next day to see how I was doing.

I think what I find the most remarkable is that Diane came by her kindness the hard way—through a difficult childhood followed by 28 years of abusive marriage before she managed to escape with her two children and her life. Thank God, she has been married a second time for 14 years to Ray Dillard, a man who truly appreciates her and whose kindness almost equals hers. I say "almost" because I haven't met the person whose unselfishness surpasses Diane's.

Now, don't get me wrong. She's not running around looking for people to save. Her daily routine is brimming over with responsibility, which includes loving up her and her husband's many children and grandchildren, while caring for her aging mother, who lives with her. Even so, Diane greets the never-ending stream of people through her front door with unlimited enthusiasm. She seems to have an endless store of love, which allows her to give something to everyone.

Diane even helps me with work. I've been ensconced in a book project about Holocaust survivors for the past few years that has taken its toll on me emotionally. I recently finished reading a book that was phenomenal—the kind that holds a reader rapt with anticipation. I called Diane bemoaning the fact that I couldn't possibly dream of writing such a book. I told her I felt like I was slogging through mire and was so weighed down I couldn't write a single word.

While I was bellied up to the complaint department, I also told her that I had just received yet another rejection slip from a book agent, the second such rejection in a week. I've gotten so many now that I joked I was going to either paper a wall or make a scrapbook out of them.

Diane listened patiently, and then she simply said, "That other author had a different story to tell, but you have a wonderful story to tell and you're the one to tell it." Later that day she sent me an e-mail. It was a beautiful poem, offering advice about slowing down, being grateful for what we have, appreciating each day and not rushing through life.

That's why I decided to write this column. I wanted to tell Diane that I appreciate her more than she will ever know. It just seemed fitting to make it public, because I know that I'm not alone. There are many people in this world, especially women, who may not be college graduates or become CEOs of companies but are giants at being superb human beings. They stand in the gap for their friends and families and soften the brunt of life for us, and the remarkable part is, they do it without any pay or thought of support in return.

Of course, Diane has no idea I'm writing this and will probably clobber me when it publishes. But how can she argue with my motive? Didn't she say I've got a story to tell and I'm the one to tell it? ≋

June 2003

41

Building Memories
Home improvement by a husband with a disdain for directions leads to laughter

T HERE IS A CERTAIN joy in commiserating with people who have had similar experiences, especially if there is shared anguish over a common cause. I had such a conversation recently with Randy Fitzgerald.

The Fitzgeralds have had a recent spate of trouble with plumbing gone awry and falling ceilings, which Randy has written about several times in his column for the *Richmond Times-Dispatch*. All such problems have since been patched, which left Randy, my friend of more than 20 years, without a thing to tell me — for now.

This gave me the perfect opportunity to share some of my late husband's construction antics during the years that he, our two sons and I spent refurbishing an 80-year-old farmhouse in South Hill, Va., a small town in Mecklenburg County near North Carolina.

I knew I was in trouble when I came home from work one day, stepped into the foyer and heard a power saw running. Almost afraid to venture farther, I crept into the great room we had previously created by knocking out the wall between the dining room and the living room. To my horror I saw my husband and our younger son, Jason, hip-deep in a huge hole that they had evidently just cut out in the middle of the two rooms. When he saw me, my husband silenced the saw.

Almost unable to breathe, I managed to get out a question: "Oscar, what are you doing?"

With an impish grin, my husband replied, "You said you wanted a fireplace, didn't you?"

"Yes, but I didn't say where," came my anguished reply.

"Well, now you don't have to decide," Oscar said, laughing outright.

The situation was so absurd, I had to laugh as well. After all, the floor was history. Within minutes, I had changed from my business suit and heels to a pair of jeans and T-shirt, had threaded a garden hose through the dining-room window, and was using a hoe to mix concrete in a wheelbarrow already stationed near the hole. In just over an hour, the three of us had poured the footing for that fireplace and were washing up for dinner.

Telling Randy about that stirred up memories of other unbelievable things Oscar did during the 10 years we restructured our living space, not to speak of our religion. Several incidents rank right up there with *Ripley's Believe It or Not*.

"Randy," I asked, "do you have any idea what it's like to knock down an 80-year-old chimney while you are living in the house?"

I could almost feel him grimace. At this point, Randy tentatively asked, "Have you ever watched *Tool Time* or *This Old House*?"

"Watch them?" I scoffed. "I could have written the scripts."

Although he was aggravating at times, my late husband, Oscar, who died 12 years ago this month, was truly the most talented man I've ever known. There wasn't anything he wouldn't tackle, whether he had the expertise or not. He firmly believed in one thing: Avoid all directions and do what you think works. Most of the time it did. The only thing Oscar couldn't do was lay brick. His one attempt at bricklaying left behind a "straight" patio wall that resembled a snake in transit.

Oscar's construction forays are legion. The boys and I still laugh at his unorthodox solutions, especially the uses he found for a hammer. While he was long on ideas, he was short on patience. There were times when I thought his motto was, "If I can't fix it, I'll just break it completely."

Oscar tried to surprise me one weekend by building me a dressing-room table and bookcase while I was away at a conference. The table was perfect, but the bookcase stretched from floor to ceiling and would have made me feel like Big Brother was watching as I applied mascara. Oscar could tell by the look on my face that his handiwork was a bit off-kilter. Thinking really fast, I said, "Jason doesn't have any bookcases. This will look wonderful on the far wall of his bedroom."

Each of us grabbed a side of the behemoth and started up the staircase, where we managed to lodge the bookcase squarely on top of the banister. Without saying a word, Oscar left it dangling in midair and went outside. I retreated to the kitchen. When I heard varoom varoom, I ran back into the hallway just in time to see the top of the banister go flying through the air. Oscar calmly shut off the power saw and gave me a look that dared me to speak. Once upstairs, the bookcase looked perfect, just like the knob of the banister did after the wood putty and several coats of paint were applied.

Is it any wonder that Beau, our older son, bought a copy of Chevy Chase's *Christmas Vacation* for the three of us to watch after Oscar died? It was the perfect tribute to an imperfect man who eventually decided to leave the outdoor Christmas lights intact year-round after Jason fell with a thud from the 30-foot magnolia tree one January after trying to dismantle the long strands.

Heading into the baker's dozen of years since his death, it still seems strange to celebrate Christmas without him each December. Oscar loved laying train tracks and watching *How the Grinch Stole Christmas!* The boys loved watching him. At one point during the cartoon, Oscar always laughed until he lost his breath, fell over and made this squeaky little sound that sent the boys into gales of laughter along with him.

September is another month filled with memories. My birthday is Sept. 2. Oscar's was Sept. 3, and our anniversary was Sept. 5, the combination of the first two dates. To keep things even, I guess, he died on Sept. 23, another combination of the two dates.

I don't think it was a coincidence that our first

grandchild, a beautiful little redhead with hazel eyes like Oscar's, would be born on Sept. 20, 2002. "Maggie" has a habit of spinning her chubby little hands around in circles in perpetual motion. The first time I saw her do it, I decided right then and there what I needed to buy her for her first birthday — a hammer to break something with.

Strange, isn't it, how life has a way of filling in the hard places in ways you never expected? ≋

September 2003

42

Lassoing the Black Dog
Keeping depression at bay with a little exercise

It HAPPENED AGAIN LAST night. Two hours of sleep interspersed with two hours of leg twisting and cover pulling. Finally, it was morning, bright sunlight streaking through the Venetian blinds and ushering in another Monday, with me feeling stranded.

I usually see "it" coming, but this time I was blindsided. I should know the signs by now, but when "it" comes back I'm always surprised. I can't tell you why, but I am.

Some people refer to "it" as "depression." Winston Churchill referred to it as "the black dog." Just like an animal, it seems to stalk its prey until the unsuspecting party stumbles, offering up the jugular again.

This time, as at other times, its presence galloped back when I had wavered a few days from my usual routine of going to American Family Fitness. Unfortunately, I have paid the price before for missing gym dates and would pay it again that morning, but I marked that Monday down as a red-letter day, a never-to-be-repeated-if-humanly-possible day.

I guess I've finally learned that I can't bargain with the animal, but I can keep it at bay and actually win some freedom if I do a few things to make sure the barriers to its attacks stay shored up.

My most important barrier is exercise. I learned this quite by accident a few years back when I started out a piece I was writing with: "I'm over 50, overweight and overwrought." I spent the next several months working on a routine at American Family that not only has renewed my energy but also has become my mainstay to sanity.

At the very beginning, I was inspired by my younger son, Jason, also a member at American Family, who encouraged me daily to keep going. Between his pep talks and enlisting the help of a personal trainer, within a month I was on my own and making strides that I'm still proud of. Today, five years later, I'm more determined than ever to follow my hour-long workout schedule five to six days a week, come rain or shine, feeling good or feeling blue, with work accomplished or deadlines piling up hand over fist.

Now, don't get me wrong. I'm not going to shoot myself, although there are probably a few editors and some relatives who wish I would. I've just learned, through trial and error, that exercise is the one thing I can do to ensure a steady supply of endorphins, those out-of-view miracle workers that hunker down in the bloodstream and keep a person feeling like there is a purpose to life.

I've also found that it helps to eat a good breakfast and get a dose of sunlight each day (with sunscreen, of course). Top that off with a mammoth dose of humor and counseling sessions when needed, and the concoction spells success, at least for me. While medication works for some folks, I prefer the overall feeling of well being that comes when I exercise regularly.

I can't actually remember when my first bout with depression occurred, but I think it was about 15 years ago when my husband's kidneys failed completely from complications due to diabetes.

A plastic 4-inch plug was surgically implanted into his right side, and attached to the plug was a 6-foot tube about the width of my little finger, which had a half-gallon bag hanging from the end of it. This was so Oscar could lay the bag on the floor to drain his body fluids, then hang a new bag of sterile fluids on an IV pole to master the four daily "exchanges" which supplanted his kidney function, keeping him living for three years until a transplant at the Medical College of Virginia restored complete kidney function, but I'm getting ahead of myself.

I remember bringing Oscar back to the motel where we were staying in Danville, Va., while he was introduced to peritoneal dialysis at the local hospital. That was the first time we both got a good look at the bag that would become a fixture in our lives for a very long time.

It would stay there until Oscar had several life-threatening attacks of peritonitis, which necessitated its surgical removal and the implantation of another device in his arm for hemodialysis, a second form of blood cleansing, but I'm getting ahead of myself again.

Oscar was standing in the bathroom in the Danville motel when he removed his shirt and turned to look into the mirror at the serpentine tube that would tether him to temporary life. The only reason I didn't faint was because I had to run to catch him before he hit the floor.

From then on, the depression that accompanied his diabetes and forced retirement deepened in my husband. I think I caught it by osmosis, if that's possible. And, for whatever reason, it's still with me, albeit on a much lesser plane now.

I've tried to figure it out, tried to establish a reason for my being stalked by the same malady that afflicts about 17.5 million Americans. I think it's because I had to face my husband's unexpected death in 1991, which was quickly followed by relocations and job changes, the last one just after my mother was diagnosed with breast cancer in 1993.

The move to Richmond 10 years ago to help my mother necessitated giving up my place in a master's program at Mary Washington College in Fredericksburg. I felt my life spinning out of control, but coming to Richmond has proven to be the most stable thing I've done for the last decade. I steadied myself with freelance assignments and was fortunate enough to land this column in *Richmond Magazine* more than five years ago. And even though I had to start again from scratch, I've also completed my master's degree at Virginia Commonwealth University and serve as an adjunct professor there.

Even so, recurring bouts of depression stayed with me as I helped care for my mother until her death in February 2001, followed by my father's death in March 2003. Some days I couldn't even think about writing. It was all I could do just to tie my shoes and get to the gym for my daily fix, which gave me the energy to help my parents and keep the cycle going.

When my stalwart mother became permanently disabled with a heart condition at the age of 53, she faced depression as well. She felt as if her life had ended when she had to give up her demanding job as a seamstress at Friedman-Marks, a clothing factory once located on Hull Street. Like my husband, she had lost her sense of autonomy and a great deal of self-esteem.

My mother's ill health was probably the result of obesity. Practically starved as a child during the Depression, she never stopped eating once she married my father at the age of 18. She would milk their one cow and drink the fresh cream, enjoying every drop of it, especially since my father never scolded her for the weight she gained.

When Mama was medically retired, she weighed about 200 pounds. During a subsequent doctor's visit, her physician expressed alarm that she was gaining weight again, stressing her already damaged heart. She explained it by lamenting the loss of her job, which brought on depression, which caused her to overeat.

Mama got an ultimatum: Her physician said she could continue to smoke and overeat, but she would probably die before her grandchildren graduated from high school (Jason, her youngest grandchild, was 3 at the time), or she could stop smoking, lose weight and start going to a gym. My mother took the challenge, ultimately saw Jason graduate from college and witnessed the births of two great-grandchildren before dying at 81.

Mama's new lease on life came from joining Weight Watchers, switching from cigarettes to snuff (not exactly a pretty habit, but no more inhaling smoke into her lungs), and joining a gym, which was ultimately bought out by American Family Fitness.

To this day, when I tire of exercise, I envision my mother during the last years of her life. While she was able, I took her to the same American Family that I still visit. I almost held my breath as Mama walked for 30 minutes on a treadmill, with an oxygen tube running to her nose from the tank she laid across the bow of the treadmill to offset the full-fledged emphysema she finally developed.

When she could no longer make the trip to the gym, Mama walked on a treadmill in her living room, sometimes no more than 10 minutes a day. She finally gave up about a year and a half before she died, but she always encouraged me to continue my exercise. So did Jason.

When Jason last lived with me, he owned a basset hound named Levi. That dog and I had different ideas of where he should live. Suffice it to say that I won on the day I bought a doghouse at a yard sale on my way home from church. Jason and Levi have long since departed, but the doghouse got reroofed recently along with my garage. I've thought about getting rid of it over the years, but I decided to keep it as a silent reminder that the "black dog" has found an abode somewhere else. 〰

October 2003

43

Freedom's Fighters
Doing work that's worthy of those who made it possible

LAST JUNE I was fortunate enough to have an all-expenses-paid trip to attend the Ted Scripps Leadership Training Program, a conference hosted by the Society of Professional Journalists (SPJ) in Indianapolis, Ind. I spent two-and-a-half days in intensive classes at the University Place Conference Center and Hotel, a truly wonderful spot, located smack-dab in the middle of a campus shared by Indianapolis University and Purdue University.

The final night, we attended an oath-taking ceremony. As I stood among the conference participants, each holding a lighted candle, I thought about what a privilege it is to live in a country where freedom of speech is not only guaranteed, but celebrated.

Surrounded by a group of college students, the society's future professional members, I witnessed the re-enactment of the original ceremony and joined in to repeat the antiquated verse of the pledge written long ago by 10 young men, also college students. They dedicated themselves in 1909 to journalistic endeavors and established

Sigma Delta Chi, the forerunner of SPJ. It was a moving service, made more so by the fact that all the people in that room, with the exception of a small number of staff personnel, were volunteers in the organization, and all of us shared a common privilege within our democratic society. We have the sacred trust of giving our fellow countrymen an opportunity to view as many points of an issue as possible in order to determine which side they want to uphold.

The first morning of the conference, I went for some exercise and tried to find the Canal Walk, reputed to be a gorgeous site running through the middle of the city. Unfortunately, I had been given the wrong directions, so I ran out of time and had to hotfoot it back to the conference.

I set out again early the second morning. After several blocks I saw a lanky young man running toward me in black spandex shorts and a green tank top, his cornrows flopping jauntily. I held up my hand, and he slowed to jog in place, reassuring me that I was, in fact, going the right way. Just as he went out of sight, I spied the Canal Walk. I eagerly descended two long flights of granite stairs and hastened down by the water, where an older man was helping a little boy coax ducks toward them with breadcrumbs.

I picked up my pace and got lost in the beauty of the spouting fountains, purple coneflowers and orange trumpet lilies, each scene beckoning me farther and farther along. All at once, I realized that I was lost. Even so, I continued a few more steps.

Suddenly an imposing granite monument sprang up to the right of me. Always interested in military history, I walked up close and began to read the words etched into the huge gray slab that towered over me. It was about the USS Indianapolis, the ship that delivered the world's first operational atomic bomb to the island of Tinian on July 26, 1945, thereby sealing the end of World War II. After the delivery, the ship went on to Guam. Midway between Guam and Leyte Gulf, the Indianapolis was hit by two torpedoes fired by a Japanese submarine. What happened next is detailed by the monument's text:

"Of the 1,196 aboard, about 900 made it into the water in the twelve minutes before she sank.... Shark attacks began with sunrise of the first day, and continued until the men were physically removed from the water, almost five days later. Shortly after 11:00 a.m. of the fourth day, the survivors were accidentally discovered by Lt. (jg) Wilbur C. Gwinn, piloting his PV-1 Ventura Bomber on routine antisubmarine patrol.... A PBY (seaplane) under the command of Lt. R. Adrian Marks was dispatched to lend assistance and report. En route to the scene, Marks overflew the destroyer USS Cecil Doyle and alerted her captain of the emergency. The captain of the Doyle, on his own authority, decided to divert to the scene.

"Arriving hours ahead of the Doyle, Marks' crew began dropping rubber rafts and supplies. While so engaged, they observed men being attacked by sharks. Disregarding standing orders not to land at sea, Marks landed, and began taxiing to pick up the stragglers and lone swimmers who were at greatest risk of shark attack. When the plane's fuselage was full, survivors were tied to the wing with parachute cord. Marks and his crew rescued 56 men that day. The Cecil Doyle was the first vessel on the scene. Homing on Marks' PBY in total darkness, the Doyle began taking Marks' survivors aboard. Disregarding the safety of his own vessel, the Doyle's captain pointed his largest searchlight into the night sky to serve as a beacon for other rescue vessels.... Of the 900 who made it into the water, only 317 remained alive."

I walked away from the monument blinded by tears and unsure of how I'd get back to the hotel. As if previously orchestrated, the same young runner came into view again, stopped to jog in place and gave me directions again. As I walked, I thought of the untold sacrifices that so many of us don't know about. It's not only the veterans who have paid the price of freedom; it's their family members as well, suffering the agony of a lost loved one. All wars have countless unseen casualties; many of them languish in veterans' hospitals, while others walk around us unnoticed every day. I was astounded to learn a few years back that one out of every four homeless individuals in the U.S. is a veteran.

I returned to the hotel determined once again to always offer my best to the field of journalism, to leave words worth something. There are members of my profession, just as in any profession, who sully the waters for the rest of us. I can only hope that there are enough dedicated journalists who will, like the runner, take time to offer the right directions, more than once if necessary, or, like the Doyle's captain, somehow be able to shine a light just long enough to offer hope to others we'll never know.

In a letter dated Jan. 16, 1787, and addressed to Edward Carrington, who served as a colonel in the Continental Army, Thomas Jefferson wrote, "Were it left to me to decide whether we should have a government without newspapers, or newspapers without a government, I should not hesitate a moment to prefer the latter."

Lest we forget, freedom isn't free. It's a hard-earned right, paid for by the blood of those willing to serve in the armed forces. It will always remain so. On Nov. 11, Veteran's Day, I plan to set aside some time remembering the sacrifices that veterans have made so I can have the privilege to write words to honor them.

For more information on the USS Indianapolis, visit www.ussindianapolis.org. ≋

November 2003

44

Girl Power

The fine art of negotiation, as practiced by an 11-month old

I T WAS A RED-
letter day—Friday,
Aug. 8, 2003. I had
decided early on that I would
watch Dr. Phil at 3 p.m., an inexpensive reward I
sometimes give myself when I finish a job. I was
really on top of it that day. Not only had I finished
a writing assignment, I had also managed to clean
out an old file of tax receipts.

Feeling really proud of myself—even smug—I
prepared air-popped popcorn and green tea with
mandarin orange flavoring, sweetened with Equal.
I was on a roll: work done, snack in hand, no fat, no
sugar. With a glass brimming with iced tea and a
huge bowl of popcorn, I turned the TV on and
stretched out, ready for a feast and entertainment
by 2:59 p.m.

At 3:15, I'm munching and drinking and
anxious for the first commercial to be over. I
had planned to learn a lot from the day's program
lineup, during which Dr. Phil was purporting to
teach women the art of negotiation. In the first few
minutes of the show, I had heard him give an

astonishing statistic: that 46.5 percent of the women in the world pay more for goods and services than men because they lack "haggling" skills. And according to the 2002 Statistical Abstract of the U.S., in which all full-time, year-round workers are considered, I personally learned that men make an average annual salary of $31,039 compared to women, who make only $20,309. That's downright disgusting, but I digress.

Dr. Phil was just about to share his knowledge on how to negotiate a car purchase, which truly interested me, since my own car had blown an engine just a week earlier. Just when Dr. Phil was gearing up, the phone rang. Thinking it was a sales call, I tried to ignore it but couldn't.

"Good afternoon, this is Nancy Beasley," I said in my professional 9-to-5 voice.

"Well, how you doing, Mom?" my older son, Beau, asked.

"For once in my life, I'm eating popcorn, drinking tea and watching TV," I sheepishly admitted. "What are you doing?"

"I'm driving around in a Lowe's parking lot."

"You're what?"

"I'm driving around in a Lowe's parking lot."

"Don't you have anything else to take up your time?"

"Not while Maggie is asleep."

"Well, how fast are you going?" I asked, suddenly concerned that he was talking on the phone and driving with my only grandchild asleep in the backseat.

"Oh, I don't have to go very fast," he said. "I just have to keep moving."

"What happens if you stop?" I asked.

"It gets real ugly," he said, almost in a whisper.

"Well, how many times have you been around the parking lot?"

"I've lost count. Leila [his wife] is inside looking for a light fixture."

"You mean to tell me that you are driving around in circles just so Maggie won't wake up?"

"You got it. The people in the store might have even thought of calling the cops by now. I keep seeing the same sales clerks looking out the store window. They probably think I'm a pedophile."

I had given up on eating the popcorn after the first sentence or two and was laughing so hard my son asked if he should call back another time.

"No, no," I managed to squeak out. "Keep on. I need some entertainment in the worst kind of way." My son's silence told me that he didn't see the humor in the situation.

When I could catch my breath, I tried another approach. "Let me get this straight," I said. "You are 38; she's 11 months old."

"That's about the size of it."

"Aren't you supposed to be the adult?"

"Well, yes, but trust me, you don't want to wake Maggie up when she has just begun a nap. I tried that once, thinking I could gas the car and she would sleep through it, thought I could do it in about three minutes. Well, it didn't work."

"Why do you think she wakes up when you stop?" I asked between shrieks of laughter.

"There must be a switch on her butt that opens her eyes when I cut the car off," he answered sarcastically.

As if reading my mind, he said, "You need to write about this in one of your columns." And then there was silence.

"Oh, no," he finally said, "there's a Prince William County cop pulling up." After a very pregnant pause, he continued. "Phew. Must have been a fender bender." In another second, he said, "Hold on; my other line is ringing."

After another brief lapse of silence, Beau clicked back on saying, "That was Leila, calling from inside the store. She's having a hard time finding the fixture she wants."

"Did she want to know if Maggie was still asleep?

"That too."

I just had to ask: "What happens when she wakes up and you aren't driving?"

"Well, most of the time, she sucks her thumb while she's asleep. When the car slows down, the first thing she does is suck her thumb harder, and then her brow begins to furrow up. It's kind of like a bank president smoking a cigar."

At this point, I'm practically rolling off the bed, and Beau decides that I'm not the diversion he was hoping for. He mumbles something about calling me tomorrow and hangs up while I'm still laughing.

I'm really sorry I didn't get in the last word. I was going to encourage my son to keep driving so that Maggie could get her rest. At the rate she's handling the adults in her life, she ought to be able to help me negotiate a honey of a deal on a car by next September, when she'll turn 2 years old. By then, I'll bet I can teach her to say "BMW."

One more thing: Dr. Phil needs to meet my granddaughter if he thinks there are women out there who can't negotiate what they want out of life. ≋

December 2003

45

Resurrecting Old Friendships
A high-school reunion leads to a New Year's resolution

"I awoke this morning with devout thanksgiving for my friends, the old and the new."
– Ralph Waldo Emerson

HIGH SCHOOL REUNIONS USUALLY VACILLATE between two extremes: pure joy or pure dread, sometimes both at the same time. It depends, of course, on whether, as a woman, you've gained weight or, as a man, if your hair has fallen out. I won't even discuss the multiple-marriage thingamajig, which really messes up the nametags, especially when both former spouses turn up at the class reunion married to someone else.

I don't know how I got drawn into the Manchester High School Class of '63 Reunion Committee. I think it was because I write for this magazine. I believe Vern Taylor, another MHS graduate who chairs the committee, read a feature I wrote about the throes of menopause and figured I needed something more constructive to do with my time, or he saw my byline and interpreted it to read "sucker." Vern called one day, welcomed me back to Richmond, Va., after my 30-plus-year hiatus and asked me to join the committee. At our first meeting, I realized Vern's ulterior motives. He had maxed out on sentence diagramming as a student, so he needed my writing services.

For the last year, our meetings have been one of the highlights of my life. About 12 of us have gotten together to enjoy hors d'oeuvres and sometimes a cookout, but we always ended up reliving stunts, either recent or long ago, and laughing until we couldn't breathe. As one meeting adjourned and we were planning another the following week, Billy Gordon, a State Farm sales representative who usually stays pretty mum, quipped,

"Damn! We're seeing each other more now than we ever did in high school."

George "Buck" Husband, who works for Honeywell Home and Building Control, boosted the event with a generous amount of seed money. After that, Buck happily attended all the meetings, laughed at our antics and generally just grazed at the food trays. Every time we suggested sending him an e-mail with a job assignment, he'd hold up his hands and say, "Not me. I don't do e-mail."

Numerous ideas were considered for entertainment. One of the funniest came from Sally Stewart Huband. Sally, who recently retired after 32 years as a teacher, 31 of them in Chesterfield County, said, "I suggest a talent show. I want to dress up like a raisin and sing *I Heard It Through the Grapevine.* " We laughed but ignored the suggestion. After 40 years, some of us probably looked more like prunes than raisins.

Maureen Goode, an employee at the Henrico

County Social Services Department, took center stage for organization. She had all the past receipts, letters and old photos, not to mention a bunch of annuals from bygone years. Somehow, she has managed to keep us on the straight and narrow when the agenda got crowded.

Just in case you think school crowding is a new problem in Chesterfield County, think again. There were so many World War II "babies" attending classes in the mid-1960s that a swing-shift pattern had to be adopted to accommodate them all. Forget about building more schools — there were just too many of us. A compromise of sorts was reached when the decision was made for a pile of teens to attend classes between 8 a.m. and noon, and a second shift would end at 4 p.m., thereby turning Old Broad Rock School, an unused elementary school, into a multiple-use dwelling.

My friend Sally Huband's mother was furious about the decision. In a loud voice, she announced, "The damn county has nailed two boards together, called it a school, and suddenly it's not condemned anymore."

Sally and I were in the first shift at Old Broad Rock. I can't even remember if the second shift had the same teachers or not, but we all took history, English, science and mathematics. No art, music, physical education, shop or home economics, and I can't remember any school clubs either.

As you might imagine, a good deal of our committee time has been devoted to finding lost classmates or deciding whether some of them were, in fact, still alive. Vern sent an e-mail to the committee just a few weeks before the Oct. 11, 2003, reunion. The subject for the e-mail was "RESUR-RECTION," and it read like this:

"Gang: Mark Guy would like to be removed from the deceased list. He was at Shoney's restaurant tonight insisting that he is alive, and since his wife confirmed this, I am willing to change the database."

Right after joining the reunion committee, Vern told me about another group of MHS graduates who meet regularly on the second Thursday of every month. Carolyn Jenkins Matthews, class of '62, came up with the bright idea after getting in touch with some old friends she'd known since the age of 6. Billy Cecil, also class of '62, and several others helped jump-start the tradition about three years ago. It has since developed into someone always reclaiming a lost friend over dinner. It was a hoot to learn that all those gray-haired folks attended Manchester at one time and to realize I hadn't accidentally stumbled into an AARP meeting.

I will never forget the first MHS class reunion I attended in 1983. My late husband, Oscar, said he wouldn't know anyone there and was reluctant to attend. He finally relented, but I warned him to be on the lookout for a beautiful, Amazon-sized woman who would descend on me, probably bodily pick me up and scream, "Wright Baby, where you been?" That would be my dear friend, Gina Welton Vaughan, one of the daughters of "Bootsie" Welton, a beloved Chesterfield County police officer.

Minutes into the reunion, I spotted Gina swooping toward me. Suddenly she stopped, turned to my husband and said, "Oscar, what in the hell are you doing here?" Seems Gina and Oscar worked for the same firm, she in Lynchburg and he in South Hill. They had met years earlier. Needless to say, Oscar felt right at home.

This is a new year just ripe for resolutions. If you're like me, I always have good intentions to get in touch with former friends. Some folks say the road to hell is paved with good intentions.

I don't know about you, but I'm making that call today. ≋

January 2004

46

Helping Hands
These women are true homemakers

A KALEIDOSCOPE OF AUTUMN leaves fell around the construction site at 313 Crawford St., their colors complementing and blending with an orange work trailer, yellow scaffolding, and green and blue Porta-Johns just off to the side of the work area.

The framework for the unfinished house had just been set, the last side having been raised by a clutch of black and white hands, some manicured, some rough, both big and small, experienced and novice. There were only four men on site, supervisors for a gang of women dressed in white T-shirts. The shirts had a sketch of a green hard hat on the front. Names of several local women's clubs encircled the hat, which also had the silhouette of a white house drawn on it. Sweat rings formed on some of the participant's shirts, while others seemed nonplussed by the exertion. Regardless of sweat equity, most of them (even one of the men) were wearing earrings along with their tool pouches and heavy-duty shoes.

Leisha LaRiviere, the spark plug for the project,

quipped, "My slingbacks came from Nordstrom's and my work boots from Wal-Mart." It was one of many funny incidents that cemented the "Women Building a Legacy" project, the first female-only-built house in Richmond spearheaded by local women's groups working in conjunction with Richmond Metro Habitat for Humanity.

Kathy Garvin, executive director for the local affiliate of Habitat for Humanity International, described her organization as an ecumenical Christian housing ministry that works on the premise of building "simple, decent and affordable housing in partnership for those in need."

Richmond Metro Habitat offered needed guidance and support throughout the project and was responsible for identifying the build site and the homeowner, Mary Young, who worked at other Habitat building sites, as well as her own, and completed training courses on finance and home ownership.

Garvin, one of the few southpaws on the job, stopped hammering long enough to say, "This was Leisha's idea, although she hasn't liked me to talk much about that part of the project."

LaRiviere presented the idea for "Women Building a Legacy" to the board of directors and membership of the Junior Federated Women's Club of Chester when she was president of the organization in 2002-03. Through relentless networking, that group's membership spread out and enlisted countless others before ending up with $50,000 and other amenities donated to the project. Some of those donating were LeClair Ryan Professional Corp. and the Junior League of

Richmond, which supplied a $5,000 grant, provided 60 members' worth of "woman power" at the work site, and led the public relations effort for the build.

At 7:30 a.m. on the first "build day," participants picked up their tools and stood in line waiting for their names to be written on masking tape with magic markers. The tape was then pressed to the back and front of their T-shirts, so the supervisors would know to whom they were speaking. At the job's completion, the nametapes would be removed and proudly slapped in place on the work trailer, joining hundreds of other volunteers' names from past Habitat projects.

Project supervisor Bill Erhart, who has worked in construction for 25 years, looked like a model for a Swiss Alps catalog on Nov. 3, the first day of the 10-day blitz-build started last year. He wore a broad-brimmed hat along with a red T-shirt, which was partially covered by a strapped harness contraption in place over his shoulders.

I asked Erhart if supervising the 400 female workers needed for this project would be tantamount to bagging air. He laughed before saying, "No, not really, I prefer women as volunteers. Men come out thinking they know how to build when, in fact, they might not. I always get nervous when a guy arrives with a brand-new nail apron." He leaned forward and added, "The thing about women is, when you tell them something, they listen."

The ping of the hammerheads finding nails mixed with the thud of sledgehammers slowly nudging walls into place as I walked around the house's perimeter, dodging mud puddles left over from a recent rain. Without warning, I was suddenly covered from head to foot with sawdust. Dr. Cora Salzberg had lowered the handle of the miter saw she was using several feet away, oblivious to my presence. It reminded me, as if I needed reminding, that this was a serious work site.

Salzberg, a Richmond resident and national officer of The Links Inc., was the catalyst behind the Richmond Links affiliates' involvement. The nonprofit organization is made up of more than 10,000 women of African descent dedicated to sustaining cultural, civic and educational programs for African-Americans. The Commonwealth, James River Valley and Richmond chapters donated $37,000 to the project and also provided food for seven out of 10 building days.

Salzberg said, " This was a time to step up to the charge and make real our mission of community service through collective efforts."

Young, the new homeowner, is a single parent who works full time as an assistant counselor for Richmond Residential, an organization that provides permanent housing for the mentally disabled, while also attending J. Sargeant Reynolds' nursing program full time. She will take possession of the house this spring and started planning a housewarming party in January before the final inspection was complete.

"It's impossible to describe how I feel," she began. "So many positive things have happened since I've been in this program. I knew this house was going to be perfect because women built it. When I first learned that I was to be the recipient, I was happy and scared, too. I've never been a homeowner; it's a lot of responsibility. I'm going to have a party anyway when I move in. I'll just have a house full of people, especially sponsors. I can't thank them enough."

Young said her daughters, Simone Young, 14, and Essence Hargrove, 8, helped with some of the painting. Others were also involved: Twenty-one volunteers from the all-girl sixth-grade teams at Bailey Bridge Middle School in Chesterfield County prepared lunch for the 40 workers on the last build day. While their families donated food, the girls prepared the sandwiches, decorated the lunch bags and stuffed them. Club members discovered encouraging notes tucked inside the bags, alongside apples, oranges and cookies.

There was little doubt that another generation of young women had begun to build a legacy of their own. Other groups who helped with the project include Midlothian Jack and Jill, River City Express Network, and the North Central Kiwanis Club. ≋

March 2004

47

Anything But Average
Changing mixed messages to women, one magazine at a time

"My father left Christmas day when I was 12. He took his education and his money with him," Rebekah Pierce states matter-of-factly. "My mother had four children and a high school education. She had always wanted to go back to school, but my father always had an excuse why she couldn't."

Pierce's mother worked four jobs to support her children and still works as a nurses' aide today.

"We lived in shelters, in a car. My mother was courageous, even when the sheriff kicked us out of our house. She would tell my sister and me to get our education first and worry about a man later."

Pierce followed her mother's advice, dividing her attention between San Francisco State University and the military, where she met Elehue Pierce at Langley Air Force base. They were married in 1999.

"Unfortunately, my brothers joined gangs and ended up in jail," Pierce explains. "Both are fine now and have families. My sister got a master's at Old Dominion University and is a counselor for troubled children."

Pierce, now 31, has also utilized her education to help young people. Along with teaching, she is the self-appointed editor-in-chief of *Average Girl Magazine*, an enterprise she started as an online publication in June 2003.

All in one breath, Pierce says, "Besides the magazine, I have a 2-year-old son, (and I) teach at Virginia Union University and at J. Sargeant Reynolds (Community College) in their dual-enrollment English programs at Hanover and Atlee high schools."

She also adds that she is a candidate in a doctoral program at the Virginia Commonwealth University Department of Education.

That's how I heard about Pierce. As an adjunct instructor at VCU, I'm privileged to receive e-mails about the goings-on there. Recently I received an e-mail asking for volunteer writers for Pierce's magazine.

"I wanted to change the way the media targeted young girls and women," Pierce explains. "I got tired of passing magazine stands and seeing '101 Ways to Kiss Your Boyfriend,' 'How to Be Hot and Sexy.'"

Pierce's classroom experience also jolted her during her first year of teaching.

"I had students with babies due the week before mine," she says in an exasperated tone. "I remember thinking, 'I'm 28, married, pregnant, but I'm still scared, even with an education.' My students were 14 and 15, had little education, weren't married, pregnant. They thought they didn't need school because this man was going to take care of them."

A familial situation hit even closer to home.

"My cousin was attacked by the father of the child she was carrying. The child survived. My cousin lived four months in a coma. At her funeral I heard how my cousin loved children because this was her seventh child. I remember thinking it was about her not finding something in herself to love and thinking a man was going to do it for her. I don't think she realized until the end that you can't love yourself through the eyes of somebody else."

Pierce turned to prayer for a solution to her troubled thoughts.

"I'll never forget it," she says quietly. "I was lying in bed staring at the ceiling. All of a sudden 'Write a magazine' came into my head. I said out loud, 'What? What in the world would I call it?' God said, 'Average.' "

Pierce believes that the name is perfect for her mission.

"Average is not a bad thing," she explains. "I wanted to offer young women an avenue showing them it's OK not to be the prettiest or wealthiest girl on the block."

While attending school in Stockton, Calif., Pierce always felt like an outsider. Although she has beautiful, creamy skin, she was teased for not wearing makeup, for having a "roly-poly neck." She even broke her glasses in the fifth grade when an advertisement aired claiming that girls with glasses didn't need boyfriends.

"My mother couldn't afford new glasses. I had

to go to school with them taped in the middle.

"When I was in high school, there were times we wore the same clothes for two years. Some days we had nothing to eat or made pancakes out of flour and water. My friends were driving cars, had parents and money. I was teased for not having good hair, for wearing glasses. I spoke very properly. I went to class every day, did my homework and knew the only way I was going to get out of there was through education."

She continued, "I saw girls like me getting pregnant, on welfare, as addicts, killing themselves. When I looked back, I said, 'I need to name my magazine Average Girl, for the girl with big dreams and goals.' Because she doesn't fit a certain image, society wants to tell her that she is not good enough. It's to provide 'average' girls and women with informative, motivational and inspirational articles and resources that work to heal the heart, mind, body and soul."

Pierce says her mother has been pushing subscriptions since she began publishing the magazine, which is currently a print-to-order affair. She has reconciled with her father, who also supports her work.

"I have 18 subscriptions now," she says proudly. "It's $24 a year."

Pierce is bearing the entire cost of the print version of the magazine, which she started last December after averaging 400 hits a month on her Web site. At the magazine's inception, Pierce felt her old high-school fears coming back.

"I had to sit back and say, 'Wait a minute. I do

have something: ambition, a talent for writing, and I know this needs to be out there. If God wants it to be, I just have to make sure I'm in the position for him to let things work out.' "

That's when she put out the call for writers to VCU.

"I got six women right off the bat."

Pierce's cadre of writers includes one male. She dreams of a time when she can pay them. Before that, though, she needs a publisher to help foot the bills.

"The magazine is just the beginning. I have designed a journal and a handbag. Proceeds will go to a charity for women and children."

Pierce needs the magazine to succeed to move on to the community events she has planned.

"I have no intention of this failing—financially, spiritually, or otherwise," she says. "I believe average girls can do extraordinary things." ≋

April 2004

48

Southern Hospitality
A visit to the tropics reveals some familiar friendliness

"Broad, wholesome, charitable views of men and things cannot be acquired by vegetating in one little corner of the earth all one's lifetime."
– Mark Twain, *Innocents Abroad*

As my younger son, Jason, said to a friend one day, "My mother's mind has taken her places she'll probably never go." This past November, my mind met up with reality, when I flew to the Caribbean for a sailing trip aboard the Royal Clipper, the largest sailing vessel in the world.

After arriving in Barbados, I spent the first night in the Savannah Hotel. When registering, Abram Alleyne, the hotel manager, overheard me asking if vegetarian dishes were available in their restaurant. He introduced himself and said he just happened to have some homemade conkie, a veggie Barbados delicacy, in his office. Within minutes Alleyne produced a sample of the dish, which is traditionally served on Nov. 30, the day Barbados gained its independence from Britain in 1966.

A mixture of shredded sweet potato, pumpkin,

coconut, butter, sugar, essences of vanilla and spices is shaped into a log-like bar, wrapped in banana leaves, tied with string and steamed. It was heavenly, like a spicy pumpkin pie at Thanksgiving.

From my private patio, I caught a glimpse of the much-celebrated white sands, the tall palm trees and the azure ocean's edge, which I couldn't wait to get my toes in.

The next morning I ventured to a nearby park, where hordes of people were practicing military drills. I got brave and asked a nicely dressed gentleman standing nearby to explain. He flashed a sparkling smile and said it was practice for their upcoming independence celebrations. I told him it was my first venture to the Caribbean and I had hoped to see an "insider" view of some of the islands but didn't know a guide.

"I'm retired," he said. "I'll drive you around if three hours is enough."

For a moment, I hesitated. I don't know whether I agreed because of his genuine hospitality, which reminded me of my own Southern heritage, or because, although dressed immaculately, he was barefoot.

When he said, "I'm Errol—like Errol Flynn," I knew I had a winner.

As we whizzed by banana plantations with the trees hanging full, I saw former sugar-cane factories and fields of sweet potatoes growing and listened as Errol described how it took a very practiced harvester to dig the potatoes that sometimes weighed six pounds. I nodded, remembering how my Daddy used to get on his knees and carefully lift white potatoes out of the crumbly ground with his hands so as not to bruise them. Daddy would have loved the tour and the glimpses of singular cows and goats tethered alongside the modestly built houses.

I held my breath as Errol raced around hairpin curves and laughed as he "beep-beeped" the horn incessantly, not only a warning that another vehicle was approaching, but as a "howdy" to friends.

"Everyone knows me from when I was a postman," he explained.

I laughed out loud from sheer joy. I couldn't believe a girl who grew up milking cows in Southwest Virginia was actually touring a far-flung tropical island and learning how similar their agricultural practices were.

I was greeted with a rum punch when I stepped aboard the Royal Clipper that afternoon. Since I don't imbibe, I went to my cabin and unpacked.

I was like a kid in a candy shop as I checked out the three decks, three swimming pools, gym and massage area, piano bar, and the tropical bar, not to speak of the exquisite dining area, which is reached via a spiral staircase agleam with polished brass and mahogany. I became Scarlett O'Hara in *Gone With the Wind* every time I descended the lushly carpeted steps for dinner.

Over the next seven days, I found myself running from starboard to port and craning my neck to see the top of the 197-foot mast above the crow's nest. (Now that I'm a seasoned traveler, I can use those terms.) Brave clients were allowed to sit in the crow's nest after stepping into a harness-like contraption and climbing the ropes, assisted by the sailing crew. While I didn't climb, I did venture into the hammock-like netting strung alongside the bowsprit. For several magic moments, I was suspended somewhere between heaven and the bluest teal water I've ever seen. Watching the sails billow like huge magnolia blossoms and swimming at midnight under a star-studded cobalt sky were added treats, as was the white-uniformed captain playing bagpipes on deck at dusk.

The gregarious way the waitstaff jested with each other added pleasure to each day. Their melodious dialects—representing 29 nationalities (each could also speak English)—dipped and swayed with the swells carrying the tall ship to the exotic ports of the Grenadines, Grenada, Tobago Cays, St. Vincent, Bequia, St. Lucia, Marigot Bay, Martinique and back to Barbados.

One waiter in particular, Laurentiu Olingheru of Romania, stood out above all the rest. He flawlessly served full plates and removed silverware as delicately as if he were directing an orchestra. His ramrod stature and reserved demeanor made me want to crack through to the person beneath the formality. And so, when he was taking dessert orders one evening—the devil made me do it—I ordered a green bean salad. Seconds later, the entire table, including Laurentiu, exploded in laughter. It was a turning point. The next morning, he greeted me with a huge smile and warmly told me of his family and homeland at my request. He approached my table that evening with his hand outstretched, palm turned downward, placing a photo of his beautiful 2-year-old daughter in my palm. We both got misty-eyed as he talked of her, his wife and his mother.

I had yet another surprise waiting. After disembarking from the Royal Clipper, I took a taxi into Barbados hoping to find a souvenir book with photographs of the islands I had visited. Successful at that, I entered a restaurant inside the department store, where I asked a stunningly beautiful native woman (obviously a manager) about the menu. She suggested flying fish accompanied by coo-coo, a mixture of cornmeal, okra, onion and garlic that's similar to grits. I was enjoying the meal when she came to ask how I was faring. She was so effervescent, I couldn't help telling her about the lovely manager at the Savannah Hotel, and how nice he was to offer me the conkie.

Grinning from ear to ear, she said, "I made the conkie. That's my husband." ≋

May 2004

49

Growth Spurt
A family counts its blessings as they come, through adoption or otherwise

Isaac Hanrahan, 5, can be very convincing.

"Daddy," he said recently in a phone conversation, "there's a little baby in Mississippi. His name is Joseph, and I think he's my brother."

Tom Hanrahan, a father of five, is somewhat used to getting unique calls from his children at work. It probably helps keep him on his toes as a staff attorney doing research for judges sitting on the federal bench, a position he has held for the past 11 years.

Tom and his wife, Jen, are both 37 and both deeply in love with each other and parenthood. Their house, located on Grove Avenue in the Fan, seems to blend in well enough with the neighborhood of restored homes in that area. The interior, though, resembles what could easily be characterized as a Dr. Seuss playpen, beginning with the multicolored stool tops in the kitchen and the multicolored walls plastered with art by the Hanrahans' multicolored children.

Jen and Tom married when they were 27, not long after they met while attending classes at William and Mary law school. Jen worked briefly as an attorney but then began teaching at Benedictine High School. Of late, she's been a stay-at-home mother who home-schools their children.

Unsuccessful at natural pregnancy, the Hanrahans sought medical help, also without success, for over a year. Finally, they attended a 1997 seminar on adoption offered by the Children's Home Society, a 102-year-old adoption agency that has placed more than 10,000 children since its inception.

"The meeting helped us learn about options and that domestic adoptions aren't that expensive," Jen says. "We spent a lot of time deciding on what we could handle and then turned in our list to the agency. Our parameters were age 4 and younger and any racial background."

The Hanrahans had no way of knowing what a landslide they had set in motion. They were called within three days of their home study, an investigation of prospective parents conducted by the adoption agency.

There are two ways to adopt. The first, an agency adoption, occurs when a child is available for adoption, in either a foster home or when legal rights are terminated. The second method is a parental placement.

"This happened to be a parental placement," Jen explains. "Our home study was done on a Thursday, and on Friday Isaac's biological mother walked into the adoption office and picked our picture out of a book."

Isaac's mother was five-and-a-half months pregnant. The Hanrahans went along on her remaining medical visits and were both present at the birth. Isaac, who was born May 5, 1998, knows he is adopted and visits with his biological mother, usually by phone.

That first adoption seemed to set a pattern. The Hanrahans, who attend Harvest Renewal Church, a multiracial organization in the Virginia Commonwealth University area, were in their social worker's office for a visit when they were asked if they might know anyone interested in adopting a 3 1/2-year-old African-American girl.

Jen recalls, "We got outside, looked at each other and said, 'She's ours.' "

The Hanrahans waited while the agency tried to place the child with an African-American family, but two months later they drove to a Roanoke Children's Home Society foster home to collect their daughter, ZayAnna, whose name they short-ened to Anna.

And then there were three.

"Anna came home in December 1999," Jen says. "In January, I thought I had this knock-down, drag-out flu. I couldn't keep anything down. I packed Isaac and Anna into the car during a blizzardy day and drove to the drugstore where we lived in Church Hill. I had been looking at the drugs and ended up in front of the pregnancy tests."

Just as a precaution, Jen bought a test. The positive results brought tears of joy. She called Tom but was overwhelmed with emotion.

"I handed the phone to Anna and said, 'Here, talk to Daddy.' Anna goes, 'Mommy just peed on a stick and now she's crying.' "

Mary was born in September 2000, which meant a move or a home expansion was in order. The Hanrahans found their current 3,600-square-foot home, which at the time was in need of extensive repair.

"When we moved into this house, it was a wreck," says Tom, who did much of the renovation himself. "We had a 1-year-old, a 2-year-old and a 5-year-old. We have pictures of them running around in mud pits in the back yard."

Eventually Jen resigned from Benedictine, just in time for another home study. A social worker checked out the couple's marriage, their finances and the status of the current children. A few days later, they received a call about a 15-month-old girl. They were thrilled to learn her name was Sarah, a name they had already chosen for a girl. (They had decided on Joseph if they ever adopted another boy.)

Sarah and Mary are 11 months apart and shadow each other's every move in a beautiful portrait of contrasts. Sarah has flawless caramel skin, brown eyes and four pigtails that sit perkily atop her head. Mary has porcelain-like skin, straight, wheat-colored hair and green eyes. They are inseparable. Sarah was born in 2000 and adopted in December 2001.

And then there were five.

Jen's sister-in-law in Mississippi called to say they had fallen in love with a little 3-month-old African-American boy named Joseph in their church whose first adoption had fallen through. Coincidentally, Tom and Jen's most recent home study was the next one that hit that social worker's desk.

"God must think we were really dumb," Jen says with a bubbly laugh. "It's like we don't know if they're ours unless they came with [biblical] names we had already picked out."

That's when Isaac called to suggest that Tom claim his brother.

Watching the cluster of children, so different in so many ways, is awe-inspiring. While Anna, already a genteel lady at 9, quietly makes cookies and hot tea for a guest, Isaac is a veritable jack-in-the-box, alternating between playing a computer game and making faces at Joseph, who lounges wide-eyed in Jen's arms. Nearby, Sarah and Mary play like two kittens tumbling on the floor as the phone rings intermittently.

Phone calls seem to play an awfully important role in the Hanrahans' life. Just prior to my writing this column, my own phone rang. It was Jen Hanrahan saying that she was pregnant.

And then there were six. ≋

June 2004

50

Rags to Riches of a Different Kind
Stitching up the wounds of domestic violence

"HOPE STARTED WEAVING for us in the fall of 2000," Lynn Bryant says. "I can still see her sitting in the courtyard of Magnolia Market. It was a cool November day. I kept going to check on her. I was afraid she'd bolt and try to go back home."

Hope isn't the woman's real name. If I use her real name, her husband may kill her. Those are her words, not mine, dramatically portraying what some individuals deal with long after they've fled a domestic-violence situation.

Enter Lynn Bryant.

Bryant, a faculty member at the Virginia Commonwealth University College of Humanities and Science for 15 years, relocated to North Carolina's Outer Banks in 1986 after an early mid-life crisis.

"I planned to work at the community college, live by the sea and write murder mysteries."

Instead, Bryant applied for the executive

director's position at Outer Banks Hotline, a crisis-intervention center that also includes a women's shelter.

"I'm an educator," Bryant adds, as if that explains 17 years of 24-hour on-call duties and unimaginable patience. Statistics reveal that individuals, male or female, usually leave domestic-violence situations an average of six times before they actually do so permanently.

Bryant can tell stories that would break your heart, but she prefers to focus on what she calls "dazzling successes," like Hope, whose husband finally agreed to move and stop badgering her.

"Well, he didn't," Hope says quietly. "He banged on my door at 4 a.m. every single night, stalked me, came with a gun. That was probably after the fifth time I had gone back to try and live with him. When that happened and I realized the police could not—would not—protect me, I decided to come to Hotline and let them lead me in a different direction because I couldn't help myself. I knew if I stayed there I'd probably die."

Eight months later, Hope was still deeply depressed. Bryant felt compelled to act and suggested she weave.

Enter Rabiah Hodges, the weaving director and founder of Endless Possibilities, an intriguing shop located in Manteo, just a stone's throw from the Roanoke Sound. Hodges used to work near a Hotline thrift store and noticed that discarded clothing from the store was filling up Dumpsters.

"I thought, 'Weaving classes and their materials can get very pricey. What if I use a rag-weaving concept to lower the class fees and help Hotline recycle some of the clothing they can't sell?' "

Hodges experimented with cutting clothing into strips and weaving rugs, among other things. Thrilled with the results, Bryant could foresee Hotline developing a cottage industry and establishing a safe environment for clients — the perfect way to recycle discarded clothing along with people's lives. The weaving project began in February 2000 in a warehouse behind a Hotline thrift store located in Kill Devil Hills, with all proceeds going to support the intervention programs. Hodges explains the shop's name: "One day I said, 'In weaving terminology, one yarn is called an end. So what about Endless Possibilities?' It brings the whole pun of weaving in with the concept that we can make anything with the stuff we're getting."

Enter Malcolm Fearing, an entrepreneur who offered space in Magnolia Market and now in the Fearing Building on Budleigh Street, both for nominal rent. A huge storefront window, flanked by two wooden chairs with rag seat covers hanging on entry posts, entices curious shoppers. Inside, the tall ceilings, cedar walls and soft track lighting show off woven wares — hats, pillows, scarves, rugs, carryall bags, table runners and more in a stunning array of colors and designs. Between five and 55 volunteers, men and women alike, some from Richmond, Va., donate their weaving talents to the shop each week. Standing among the beautiful byproducts of 16 looms gave me an overwhelming sense of well-being. An almost palpable calm settled over me. My experience, I'm told, isn't unusual.

"People in the Richmond area have a fondness

for the Outer Banks," Bryant says. "Vicki Powell, a wonderful woman and huge supporter of ours, offers our work on consignment at her shop, What's in Store [at 5706 Patterson Ave.]."

Like Hope, a few of Hotline's domestic-violence clients have become paid staff as weavers, instructors and seamstresses at Endless Possibilities, where classes are offered for free or at very reasonable prices.

Hodges even set up a program in Cape Hatteras Secondary School in which students, including some children with disabilities, are weaving. Their material is turned into products at Endless Possibilities, taken back to the school for "show and tell," and often sold there. Hodges also shared her expertise for similar programs in Virginia and elsewhere in North Carolina.

Still, the economic struggle is nearly as tough as the emotional one.

"This whole project of programs, recycling, renewal is very difficult to market," Bryant explains. "We're very successful with getting grants for other things—but not this. Domestic violence is so powerful, so prevalent. It's hard to put something so wonderful and positive together with it; it doesn't seem like a good fit. It's almost like bad manners to be happy when you're in the middle of being sad.

"What our clients had before may seem torn to shreds and broken, but there's always a possibility of remaking that into something else. It may not be the same, but it can be more beautiful and more useful. That's the image of this organization. It was like that with Hope. She was this big, empty shell, but as the rug grew that first day, so did her self-esteem and determination. This is such an important project, because it heals."

"Lynn forced me to come over here," Hope offers. "I was like, 'Weave, what are you talking about, weave?' I was so sad, depressed, angry, disappointed, grieving. I came because I didn't know what else to do. I just fell in love with it. It made me calmer, slowed down my thought process, made it orderly. It was instant gratification to see something beautiful being made by my own hands, out of something old that was going to be thrown away. I felt like I should be thrown away, hopeless, useless, torn apart. This project saved my life; Lynn saved my life. She was my divine intervention.

"I have seen miraculous things happen here. People feel the wonderful energy in this place. Now I feel like a whole person, like I have something to give. I think I was brought here in this place for a reason, and that was to help and to share."

Enter Hope. ≋

July 2004

51

Say What?

Getting a hearing aid can open up a whole
new world of sound

WHILE I ACCEPTED THE
necessity of glasses in 1985,
learning I needed a hearing
aid just seven years later was
another story.

Dr. Douglas Bryant, a
Richmond audiologist who
later became one of the founding partners at the
Hearing Clinics of Virginia, delivered the
bad/good news.

Bad: "You have a significant hearing loss."

Good: "Hearing aids will help."

It seemed simple. It wasn't. At the time, hearing
aids resembled a blob of beige bubble gum in the
ear tethered by tubing running from the aid around
the top of the ear to a large amplifier/microphone
behind the ear. Although I had enough hair to cam-
ouflage it, the size of the amplifier/microphone
caused my ears to flare out, similar to a miniature
school bus with stop signs extended.

My first day with amplified sound was unfor-
gettable. When I ate lunch, the noise made me
think of bulldozers excavating inside my head, and

typing sounded like a herd of buffalo stampeding over my keyboard. When I relieved myself (well, it is a part of life), I felt like I was in the midst of Niagara Falls.

By the following morning, I was more acclimated to exterior noise and deep into writing a story when I suddenly heard what could only be described as a rushing, mighty wind. Terrified, I tried to remember what to do in the event of a tornado.

"Get into the bathtub," said a voice inside my head. "Cover yourself with a mattress."

"I can't move a mattress by myself," I answered aloud.

"Cushions might work," said the voice.

As I ran toward the couch, the wind suddenly subsided. I returned to my desk wondering if I'd had too much caffeine. Twenty minutes later, the tornado started up again. Braver this time after having survived my first encounter, I inched down the hall and heard—really heard—the fan on the furnace running for the first time in my adult life.

After becoming familiar with sounds heretofore unheard, like the buzz from fluorescent lights and the hum of my refrigerator, I opted for quiet again and began wearing just one hearing aid selectively, usually when I conducted an interview.

Dr. Frank Butts, my current audiologist, understands exactly how I feel. Butts has worn two hearing aids since 2000, the result of attending a Bob Seger concert with his teenage son.

"The concert was great but louder than I ever anticipated. I didn't wear earplugs," Butts says. "The next day I couldn't hear my patients as well."

It was a transforming experience for Butts, giving him an insider's understanding of his patients. He has, during my office visits, described personal incidents that seemed funny after the fact but were disconcerting when fresh.

I can relate. Shortly after the delivery of my first hearing aid, I had an interview scheduled, part of a yearlong research project that ultimately involved talking with several individuals in the medical profession. I arrived for my appointment with a pediatrician. She wasn't in her office when I arrived, so I asked her assistant to help me move the chairs a bit closer in order to augment my hearing. When the doctor entered the room, I explained the furniture situation and asked if I could tape the interview, also to support my hearing.

Before I could even finish my request, the pediatrician screwed her face into an awful contortion, literally put her nose within inches of mine and shouted, "Well, I guess that means I'll have to talk louder then!"

Stunned, I sat in silence for a few seconds. Then I became quite philosophical. I asked, "If I were blind, would you stick your fingers into my eyes to help me see better?"

Taking the opportunity of the pause that followed, I asked, "Shall we start again?"

Butts has an explanation for such situations.

"We have accepted glasses culturally and understand that a person wearing glasses can see. Glasses have even become a fashion statement. When you see a person with a hearing aid, we assume they cannot hear. Hearing loss doesn't have to be a runaway train that ends in deafness."

He emphasizes three things in understanding hearing loss:

1) *Obtain proper evaluation and treatment from a qualified audiologist. He stresses "proper" and "qualified" and strongly encourages avoiding individuals who aren't medically trained to diagnose and treat hearing loss.*
2) *Accept the hearing loss as part of life.*
3) *Encourage others to accept it as well.*

While his advice is a bit late for my encounter with the pediatrician, maybe I can use it on my sons. They swear I can hear them lift the lid off a cookie jar at 30 paces and wonder why I can't understand their words from another room. Butts suggested I have them say my name in order to get my attention before speaking further.

Butts, who is also an associate professor of otolaryngology at Virginia Commonwealth University, enlists another technique for offering universal acceptance of individuals with disabilities. He is on a campaign to help change the way individuals with hearing loss are perceived and refers to it as "the big push going on about using 'first-person-first' terminology." Simply put, acknowledge the person before their disability.

While admitting it seems like so much semantics, Butts points out that in former times a child with Down's syndrome was referred to as a "Down's syndrome child," as if the condition was the most important thing.

"The condition does not define the person," he

states emphatically. "We want people to think that this is a person first who happens to have a problem. Disability makes someone different, and different is not inherently bad. I try to remind my patients that they are a person first and that hearing loss is of no more real importance than the fact that they might have a little arthritis in their knees and can't run the way they used to."

Hearing that (no pun intended) was comforting to me. My knees work fine, as does my brand new itty-bitty computerized hearing aid, which is about the size of a small pencil eraser with a minuscule extension attached. The whole shebang fits into my ear canal and isn't visible to anyone else. Even though I still prefer working in quiet and wearing the aid selectively, I don't feel like I have a Volkswagen in my ear.

Now it's just a beetle. ≋

August 2004

52

Gray Matters
Lessons taken from classes at the Lifelong Learning Institute

ALTHOUGH MY BODY PARTS seem to fail me on an ever more regular basis as I get older, my mind just chugs along like the little engine that could. An insatiable reader, I'm always finding stories about places I want to visit and things I want to do. Trouble is, they're usually cost-prohibitive or at far-flung distances, so I was thrilled recently when I read a story about the newly formed Lifelong Learning Institute for Older Adults in Chesterfield County, not too far from my house.

The LLI, a new venture between Brandermill Woods Foundation, the Virginia Commonwealth University Center on Aging and several other agencies, is geared specifically to those in their "golden" years, i.e., over 50 with a few life experiences under their belt. For an annual investment of $150, members can attend an unlimited number of classes in a wide variety of college-level courses, as well as related activities. No grades are given, and all instructors and staff are volunteers. Classes are held at the Watkins Annex, a building formerly used by several schools, located at 13801 Westfield, off Midlothian Turnpike behind Sycamore Square.

I called Debbie Leidheiser, director of LLI and Brandermill Woods Foundation, to get the scoop.

"When I took over as director of the foundation about two years ago, we were looking for different opportunities for our residents," she says. "We wanted more educational opportunities and more interaction with people in the surrounding area."

That suited Don Simpson just fine. Simpson, a resident at Brandermill Woods Retirement Community, had been involved in establishing a similar learning institute at George Mason University in Northern Virginia. Simpson and Leidheiser combined efforts, finding enough part-nering interests in Chesterfield County to form a committee of about 40 people. Open house at the LLI was held Dec. 1, 2003, and classes started on March 15.

Talking with Leidheiser only enticed me fur-ther. I eagerly signed up for several classes: herbs and alternative medicine, poetry, nature photogra-phy and a few others.

I attended the class on herbs, which was very interesting, but the photography and poetry class-es, scheduled a week later, bit the dust when a for-mer herniated disk decided to speak up after 15 years of silence. This is where the aforementioned disconnect between mind and body kicks in. If my mind had won the toss, I might be writing a poem right now or photographing a field of wildflowers. But, as I said earlier, sometimes ye olde body has other ideas.

Two weeks later and somewhat on the mend, I decided to take advantage of the remaining classes before the institute closed for summer break. The schedule of classes had dwindled to just a few, including French and financial planning. I can barely say "bonjour," and you don't want to point me, a dyslexic, toward anything that remotely resembles numbers, so I opted for a class taught by Helene Wagner, founder and current director of the Virginia Screenwriter's Forum who has also worked as a Writer's Guild literary agent.

Wagner, who has had five screenplays optioned by major Hollywood production companies, will be teaching later this year at Hand Workshop Arts Center and Pine Camp Arts and Community Center, as well as volunteering again as a teacher for fall classes at LLI. She does so, she says, "because I feel very strongly about mentorship and love teaching."

Wagner's class, Exploring Mythic Story, was based on one of my all-time favorite movies, *On Golden Pond*. The gist of the film is that Norman Thayer, Henry Fonda's character, and his wife, played by Katharine Hepburn, are facing their declining years, she with grace, he with a decidedly different attitude.

The long and short of it, Wagner explained, was that movies, and books and plays, too, all have a common theme and use similar formulas for plots. If the author, playwright, director, et al, do their jobs right, participants should come away from the experience with a lesson that's applicable to their everyday lives. Made me wonder about the lesson implied in the movie *Throw Momma From the Train*, but I guess that can be addressed in a future class.

I knew *On Golden Pond* held a special message the first time I saw it some 20 years ago. I was enthralled with the two loons, sleek, mysterious birds whose lives mirrored those of the aging couple portrayed by Hepburn and Fonda. And the pull between Henry Fonda's character and the one played by his daughter, Jane, was made even more poignant because they had feuded, in real life, for years, and each was getting older as the time to resolve differences was getting shorter.

I watched the movie with several other classmates after Wagner pointed out, "A myth is a story that's more than true. Many stories are true because one person somewhere at some time lived it—they're based on fact. But a myth is more than true because it's lived by all of us at some level. It's a story that connects and speaks to us all."

My class members shared knowing glances during the familial conflict scenes, enjoying the movie's reflections of our own family idiosyncrasies.

Although the sun was shining brightly when I left the building after class, the insistent hitch in my getalong told me that I, too, would soon be facing the "twilight" years of my own life, and I wondered if I'd have the grace and fortitude my parents displayed in their later years.

I found myself still thinking about the class several hours later, which cemented what Wagner had said about the "lesson" in the movie. I remembered how my parents bore their many trials and how they approached death much the same as Henry Fonda's character did—head on, resolute and determined not to give in.

It was dark outside by the time I composed this column, and as always when I turn introspective, I think of my mother. There is no doubt in my mind that she'll be with me to the end. As I leave this earth, I'm convinced I'll hear her gentle voice encouraging me, as she did so many times.

Whenever I thought I was facing an insurmountable trial, Mama would simply say, "Sleep on it. Things always look better in the morning."

With that in mind, I plan to sign up for 20 new LLI classes this fall. With any luck and a little cooperation from my body, I should make half of them. ≋

September 2004

53

Message Received
A 12-year-old column soothes a loss and starts a new friendship

T HE WOMAN ON THE phone was sobbing uncontrollably. I'd answered the call to hear, "Is this Nancy Beasley?"

"Yes," I replied. Muffled sobs followed. Several minutes later, I said, "I'm sorry if I've offended you somehow."

"It's not that," she said. "I just read one of your articles."

That really alarmed me. As she cried softly, I took a stab at a question. "Did your husband die recently?"

"On October 6." It was then May 1, the week the woman should have been celebrating her husband's 68th birthday.

"Take all the time you need," I assured her. "I've got all day."

An hour later, Carolyn Charnock, a Tangier Island native, and I were bonded through the sudden death of a longtime spouse. My husband, Oscar, and I had shared 28 years when he died in 1991, four days after pancreas-transplant surgery. Carolyn and her husband, Charles, had been married almost 44 years when he died of a heart attack as they sat in a doctor's office, waiting for his first chemotherapy treatment for lung cancer.

While we talked, we discovered our late husbands' similarities — long-term diabetes, love of the ocean, a good sense of humor and an inordinate streak of stubbornness.

I was stunned to learn Carolyn was referring to the first article I'd written about Oscar, published in the May 1992 *Rural Living*. She still receives the magazine, now called *Co-op Living*, through A & N Electric Cooperative, which provides power to Tangier. When it published, I was working for Mecklenburg Electric Cooperative in Chase City, and my article ran in 12 other co-op magazines that month.

The piece began, "I'm 46 years old, and I'm a widow. That is the hardest statement I've ever had to make in my life — one that I keep saying to myself knowing it's true. But I'm having a terrible time accepting it. By writing this, I'm hoping that there will be a healing, or some kind of release. I also want to reach out to other widows and widowers and touch them in some simple way and to say that what they're experiencing is probably not unique but rather something that each of us must walk through at one time or another."

"I bet I read that article 10 times when it first came out, and I cried every time," Carolyn said. "I guess the Lord was preparing me."

Carolyn read the article anew, then she called Mecklenburg Electric. I had resigned in 1992, but Nancy Holbrook, a friend of mine, answered the call and gave Carolyn my number.

I just had to meet this woman who validated the belief I've held since Oscar died, that no matter how long it has been, there is a pain you simply cannot understand unless you've experienced it. As I explained in that 1992 column: "Nobody has told me what to do with the 20 or 30 pairs of socks in his top dresser drawer. Nobody prepared me for Thanksgiving, when there was no one in our family who was really practiced at carving the turkey. Sometimes I think I'm an entirely different person because all these things are so new to me."

I drove two hours to Reedville and caught the Chesapeake Breeze, a ferry that traverses the waters daily, May to October. Ferries are the only transportation to and from the tiny island of Tangier, Va., unless you count the mail boat or medical helicopter.

I chatted with Linwood Bowis, captain of the Chesapeake Breeze. Bowis became quiet after learning the purpose of my visit. Finally, he spoke of "Puge" — Charles's nickname.

"Everybody liked Puge. It takes a really special person to be liked and respected as a businessman in such a small place."

I stood on deck with wind blowing through my hair, remembering the Jamestown Ferry ride that Oscar and I had taken during our honeymoon so many years ago. I was excited to meet Carolyn but apprehensive. She admitted feeling likewise, since I wanted to write about the universality of our experience. Any reluctance evaporated during our first face-to-face conversation. I did ask what prompted her call.

"I felt you would know what I was going

through. And I wanted you to know you had been a blessing to me. I think the Lord meant for us to meet, otherwise, how do you explain me getting your number? Lisa, my daughter, started it. She's a packrat like me. One day in church, she handed me your article and said, 'I think this will help you.' "

"Our house was being air-conditioned," Lisa Crockett explained. "Boxes were stacked in the attic. I don't throw away anything unless I look at it. I gave your article to Mama, but I told her it was a 'keeper' and I wanted it back."

"I've got it somewhere," Carolyn added. "I shared it with lots of people, including my Mama, who is a widow. My Daddy drowned when he was 52, my youngest daughter's husband drowned when Caroline was just 22, and I had a 38-year-old brother who died of a heart attack. I'm always cutting things out and passing them on to people I think it will help. I think it's a ministry."

For two days, I enjoyed splitting my time between sleeping at Hilda Crockett's Chesapeake House, a bed-and-breakfast now owned by Glenna Crockett, Carolyn's sister, and her husband, Denny, and eating their luscious corn pudding, along with to-die-for yeast rolls and mouth-watering pound cake. I visited Carolyn's mother, Myrtle Haynie, now 92, and walked the beautiful white beaches with my new friend on the speck of land just three miles long and a little more than a mile wide where about 700 folks live in pristine cottages.

I witnessed soft-shell crabs in different stages of undress at the crab shanty owned by Charles Charnock & Son Inc., where the Charnocks' children, including Caroline (now attending nursing school), Lisa, and Charles Jr., have assisted with the hard work for 25 years. From May through September, they either pluck crabs from the Chesapeake Bay or buy them from other watermen, place them in holding tanks, and watch them around the clock like baby chickens about to hatch. As crabs grow, they shed their shell and grow another. If not prepared for consumption immediately, the soft-as-silk crab starts to get hard again.

The visit ended way too soon. As I boarded the ferry, Carolyn handed me a gift bag and said, "Open this later." Imagine my surprise when I later discovered a sassy red brooch and several clippings, one of them the same Flavia saying I've had on my refrigerator for years. It reads, "Some people come into our lives and quickly go. Some stay a while, leave footprints on our hearts and we are never, ever the same again."

I couldn't have said it better myself. ≋

October 2004

54

Gift Exchange
Helping a friend with his Christmas shopping

A CARD SIGNED "Mary" is propped on the mantel. It reads, "Don't forget: When life gets tough, I've got a shoulder you can lean on." Inside the card is another statement: "I've got another one, too, in case it really gets tough."

John and Rita Coffman have gotten many similar cards over the past seven years, many of them, like this one, from Mary Martin, one of Rita's best friends. The cards have been steadily arriving since the Coffmans went for a walk on May 10, 1995. The leisurely stroll, during which John climbed to the third floor of a new house under construction, just to see what was happening in their neighborhood, changed the course of their lives forever.

"I went up the stairs ahead of Rita, and I really don't know what happened next," John says.

The epitome of good health and physical agility, John, then 53, fell to the first floor of the house and sustained a broken neck.

"I don't remember taking that last step, going through the plasterboard or anything. Had I realized I was falling, I would have known to throw my arms and legs out to catch a stud or a 2-by-4 or something.

"I knew I was in trouble because I couldn't move. I asked Rita to try and straighten me out because my shoulder hurt real bad. She said, 'No, I don't want to move you.' I was drifting in and out of consciousness. I remember being put in the helicopter, but I don't remember being taken out."

Following some four months at the Medical College of Virginia, John spent another year at McGuire Veterans Affairs Medical Center, where he now receives care when needed. In a strange twist of irony, the Coffmans used to visit McGuire, along with a group from St. Luke Lutheran Church. They often took refreshments to the "quads," paralyzed veterans who couldn't use their arms or legs normally.

"I have feeling from my shoulders up," John explains. "I can feel uncomfortable and, of course, can't move to do anything about it. I can't even swat a damn fly off my nose, but I do have some feeling in my bottom. It's like sitting on top of a fence post. My shoulders hurt about 90 percent of the time, and although pain medicine helps, it doesn't completely get rid of it. It would be awful without it, but there is neurological pain that medicine can't touch."

John also has pain that isn't physical. His injury not only forced him to retire as the director of media and technology at Union Theological Seminary, where he had worked for 31 years, but it made him completely dependent on others for everyday needs. He now spends his days in bed or in a motorized wheelchair with a strap around his body to keep him from falling forward. He maneuvers the chair by placing his chin into a cupped control device and answers the phone with yet another adaptation. A pencil, strapped to his left hand, allows him to use a computer, his lifeline to the outside world since the accident.

I can't remember a time when Johnny—that's what I call him—wasn't a part of my family. He and my brother, Harless, were best friends during high school and remain close today. When we were teenagers, Johnny and his sister, Bobbi Jean, and the four kids in my family were always part of the youth gatherings at Providence Methodist Church in Chesterfield County, Va. Two things stand out in my mind about Johnny: how he and my brother were inseparable and how they used to eat dinner at my mother's table and then go to Johnny's house for a second dinner. This went on for years without either mother suspecting anything.

Someone has to feed my friend now. A nurse comes three times a week to tend to bowel care, and an aide comes daily to bathe and get him out of bed, except Saturday and Sunday.

"A lot of times I'll lay in on the weekend, not only to help my bottom get some of the soreness out of it, but to help Rita. Trying to get me up is the hardest part. She is 5-foot-2-inches and weighs about 110."

John is 5-foot-10-inches and now weighs 170 pounds, after a recent loss of some 30 pounds.

This is the second marriage for both Coffmans,

who celebrated their 26th anniversary on Sept. 2. John has a son, Rita has three daughters, and they have two grandchildren. Rita worked professionally for 20 years but took early retirement from her position as a documentation librarian at Crestar Bank to care for her husband.

"What can you say about an angel?" John asks with a grin. "Every thought I have includes her in some way. That was true before the accident. I needed her before as much as I do now. She thinks about me all the time as well. I believe she knows my body better than she knows her own. I was at McGuire once and was having a terrible time. On her way out that day, she knocked on the director's door. Her exact words were, 'My husband is going to die if you don't do something.' The whole world changed after that."

Since meeting each other, the Coffmans' world has always revolved around one another, their obvious respect and love practically tangible. When asked if he thinks there is some rhyme or reason for the difficulty they've had to face, John says, "We've talked about that a lot. We think it might be because ours is a love story from start to finish. I think our friends are amazed that we are still together. From everybody that I've talked to at the hospital, a wife doesn't usually last more than a couple of months [after this kind of accident]. To show you how different she is, Rita actually gives a party every year on the anniversary of the accident. We're celebrating our survival."

Rita has helped another Coffman survive. In 1997, John's then-29-year-old son was diagnosed with non-Hodgkin's lymphoma and came home to live for about three years.

"Jay lived with us because he had to avoid pets and plants and needed air filters running 24-7," John says. "Rita had to service the filters and keep his room meticulously clean. He couldn't be exposed to chemicals of any kind, so she also had to do his laundry. He's doing fine now."

Since the accident, I have visited Johnny and Rita, but I haven't been very good at sending cards. Although Johnny has family members who can shop for him, he admits that he misses being able to personally buy gifts and cards for his wife. I thought I'd help him out with that.

"Merry Christmas, Rita. Love, John." ≋

December 2004

55

Hopes for the New Year

A desire to slow things down is Nancy's big resolution for 2005

A PRISTINE NEW YEAR IS A glorious time to kick-start fresh regimens. For instance, I plan to eat less chocolate in 2005. Actually, I resolve to only try new brands. After all, writers depend on research, don't they?

My main resolution for the coming year is simple: Slow down. Am I just imagining it or is the world on fast-forward? I pray every time I drive up I-95. I almost dread going to visit my children in Northern Virginia because I feel like I'm playing "catch me if you can" while swerving back and forth dodging cars that resemble hurtling projectiles approaching from behind. Maybe it's my advancing age. My father, who drove until he was 87, was the only person I know stopped by a state trooper and threatened with a ticket—for driving too slow.

A few months back, I had no choice but to slow things down. I was practically immobilized with the reoccurrence of an old back injury. I was lying in bed on a heating pad when the phone rang. Sally

Huband, a friend I've known for more than 40 years, heard my voice and said, "My God, you sound like you're dying. What's wrong?"

After describing my ailment, Sally announced the prescription.

"You need Earl King," she said authoritatively.

When Sally and I talked, I was limiting my trips to the kitchen, the bathroom and to see Dr. Debra Farrell, my chiropractor. Two more chiropractic sessions and four massages from King, a licensed masseur, returned me to normalcy. In fact, I was back at full tilt working practically 24/7 to make up for lost time and thanking God I had avoided surgery.

While his demeanor is genteel and comforting, King's hands became steel rods when he started the procedure that turned me into jelly. It's a good thing I'd written his check prior to the visit. Following the first session, I could barely wobble to my bedroom and slide into the comfort that only clean sheets at home can bring.

A former computer programmer, King jump-started his massage-therapy business after he and wife, Elaine (who also works with computers), became parents of quadruplets, the result of invitro fertilization in 1995. King, who is "about 50," became a stay-at-home parent by day and pursued his therapy work at night.

When asked about his calm approach to life, King says, "The spiritual side should always be the leading side of life. My work is my ministry. I pray all the time for my clients."

I may need his prayers if I'm going to achieve a more relaxed pace in my own life, given that I've just finished my first nonfiction book, *Izzy's Fire*, and am now being blessed with book signings and presentation requests. In four days recently, I drove 600 miles, gave four presentations and slept in three different beds. I don't know why, but I thought I'd just write the book and move on to another project, maybe writing about butterflies, but my life is following a path I'm not necessarily guiding any more.

Considering that, I'm also wrestling with the decision about whether to return to teaching at the Virginia Commonwealth University School of Mass Communications, my alma mater. I thought I had died and gone to heaven in May 2000 when I received my master's degree, and I was certain I was dreaming when I was offered a teaching position there two months later. Even though I was afraid to, I agreed to teach a class, but found it somehow daunting to suddenly be on the other side of the desk. When a student approached me after class one day and said, "Professor, I have a question," I turned around, sure he was speaking to someone behind me.

I have accepted a teaching assignment, but it's for only one day, a seminar at the OSHER Lifelong Learning Institute at the University of Richmond. I'll be talking about how I got into writing the book, thus dovetailing back to a subject I thought I would be leaving. I certainly never imagined I'd be teaching anyone how to write a book.

Actually, I've been teaching nursery rhymes lately and plan to do more of that in the coming year. I jump-started the slowing-down process a few months back when I carved out eight days from my schedule to help my older son, Beau, and his wife, Leila, during the arrival of their new baby. The addition of a grandson, Jeremiah Wright Beasley, who joined his 2-year-old sister, Maggie, in 2004, is another special reason to spend time just rocking, reading books like *Green Eggs and Ham*, and savoring the moment.

I will never forget the morning of Oct. 20. I had Maggie balanced on my hip, and she was blowing kisses to her parents as they left the driveway on the way to the hospital. Later that day I heated Maggie some mushroom soup, which she had never eaten before. She found it much to her liking.

At the hospital the next day, as she cuddled "Baby Jemiah" in her arms for the very first time, she leaned down, kissed him and quietly whispered a question to her 18-hour-old baby brother: "Do you like mushroom soup?" she asked in a hushed voice. My resolution to slow down had started paying off, even before the New Year.

As for Earl King, he plans to start out 2005 like other years, without resolutions.

"I don't make resolutions anymore," he says with assurance. "All I have to do is pray and ask for guidance and it will be done."

While I, too, believe in prayer, I've decided to designate 2005 as a time when I start putting myself first in line for good things, other than chocolate and coffee. Earl King is going to be one of those things. I suppose I'll have to give up my thoughts of belly-dancing lessons, though.

I'd feel funny asking Earl to pray about that. ≋

January 2005

56

Cream of the Crop
Virginia women's achievements get their due at Library of Virginia

"I am, was and always will be a catalyst for change."
— Shirley Chisholm (1924-2005), first black woman elected to Congress

W HEN I WAS A LITTLE GIRL GROWING up in the mountains of Southwest Virginia, one of my jobs was to see if any "brooding" hens had managed to incubate their eggs overnight into yellow fluff balls with toothpick-like legs. I never got over the excitement of discovering those two little dark eyes blinking at the first glimpse of light, allowing me to announce to the rest of the family that the eggs had "pipped" and would soon join the cacophony of sounds that are all part of farm life.

The "brooding" process is also part of writing. In fact, this column started incubating last spring, stimulated by my attendance at a Virginia Press Women (VPW) conference. While it's been more than 21 days (the normal time for chicken eggs to hatch), it's time to bring it to light.

Jennifer Davis McDaid, an archives research coordinator at the Library of Virginia, was one of the featured speakers at the VPW conference last April. She introduced me to a display featured at the library called "Working Out *Her* Destiny, Women's History *in* Virginia," an exhibit that will finish its run at the end of the month.

McDaid's presentation opened my eyes to the little-known history of many brave Virginia women, including those immortalized in suffrage movements in Virginia. 2004 marked the 20th anniversary of an original exhibit celebrating women's achievements. The present exhibit coordinator at the library, Barbara Batson, had always planned to have a retrospective look back and an extension at the 20-year anniversary.

The display encompasses about 40 women, including Lottie Moon (1840-1912), an Albemarle County woman who dedicated her entire life to missionary work in China. The Lottie Moon offering, for which Baptist churches almost universally collect money to support international missionary work each year, still exists.

The library's display also features Moon's older sister, Orie (1834-1883), the first Virginia graduate of the Female Medical College of Pennsylvania in Philadelphia, the oldest permanently organized medical school for women in the U.S. She eventually married John Summerfield Andrews of Tennessee and gave birth to 12 sons. The couple ran a hospital for 13 years in Albemarle County, Va., but Dr. Moon was listed on the 1880 census as "keeping house," not practicing medicine. Dr.

Edward Warren, medical inspector of the Army of Northern Virginia acknowledged that Moon was "an excellent nurse," but he also said that "no one possessing a womb or endowed with the attributes of femininity ought to dream of entering the ranks of the medical profession."

While McDaid admits respect for the societal obstacles that all women faced in earlier times, she also acknowledges a partiality to Ida Mae Thompson, a Richmond woman who kept valuable records of the suffrage movement in Virginia, aimed at gaining voting rights for women.

"She was my hero in all of this because she is the one who preserved the Equal Suffrage League (ESL) collection and brought it to the library," McDaid explains quietly.

"I believed she lived on Cherry Street, near Monroe Park. She worked as an office secretary for a doctor in Richmond, then she worked for the ESL and then for the League of Women Voters, basically working until the day she died."

Under a Works Progress Administration program, a federally funded historical-records survey in 1939, Thompson made it her personal project to ensure that suffrage records were organized. She donated them to the Library of Virginia, where her voluminous records remained in her office file drawer until 1995.

"Because it was the 75th anniversary of the passage of the 19th Amendment, there was a push to finish arranging those papers," McDaid says. She then adds, almost wryly, "Virginia didn't ratify the 19th Amendment until 1952."

A team of nine people, seven of them women,

worked on the entire display, including everything from Thompson's office files.

"We got to where we could identify her handwriting. She always wrote in pencil and she almost always wrote on little scraps of paper and backs of envelopes, never wanting to throw anything away," McDaid adds. "There were 'Vote for Women' buttons, ribbons and postcards. She was determined, writing to women in every county and city in the state and asking, 'Weren't you active in the women's suffrage movement? What do you have, and will you send it to me?'

Jessie Townsend, a big mover and shaker in Norfolk politics for women's right to vote, sent a chest full of information. Townsend's personal papers are what survived and then were incorporated into the Suffrage League collection. Ida Mae Thompson was really the hero, though. Without her we couldn't tell the story of the suffrage movement in Virginia."

McDaid, who worked as an assistant editor during part of her 14-year tenure at the library, has written about Thompson before, in the *Virginia Cavalcade*, a library publication that was discontinued during a 2002 legislative budget crunch. Part of the former exhibit was detailed in the spring 2000 issue of the magazine. The catalog for the 1984 exhibit was expanded into a book, *Share of Honor*, in 1987, written by Susan Lebsock. Plans are in the works for a revised and expanded edition of the book, to be published under a new title in 2007, so Virginia women will be part of the state's 400th birthday celebration. Lebsock, McDaid and Lori Schuyler, who also worked on the present exhibit, will share writing duties for the second edition.

"We're always looking for materials to come to the collections," insists McDaid, when questioned about the need for additional material. "We're interested in everyday women and their lives and their stories. We're hoping the current exhibit will spur donations and that it will keep people interested in Virginia women, because it's a very important part of history."

Writing this column spurred thoughts of my beloved mother, the most courageous woman I've ever known. As a child, I was always anxious to stick my finger into the layer of rich cream that formed atop the crocks that were chilling milk in the springhouse. Few things can compare to the taste of a dollop of fresh, rich cream. My mother would often say, "Try to be patient. The cream always rises to the top." ≋

March 2005

57

The Tie That Binds
Whether you're a mother or a grandmother, it's a lifetime commitment

Becoming a new grandmother has given me license to do things that otherwise would seem, shall we say, a bit on the weird side for an adult. I've always loved animals but was limited to a singular cat named Milkshake when I was growing up. I made up the difference with stuffed animals. A year after I married, my mother's threats to throw away the 32 stuffed bears, tigers, dogs, etc. I left in Richmond sent me scurrying from Chesapeake to retrieve them.

My two sons have never understood my menagerie of toys, which now, thanks to my two grandchildren—one girl, one boy—includes characters like Yosemite Sam, Cookie Monster, the Grinch, Winnie the Pooh, Snoopy and my favorite, Miss Piggy. I'm suddenly free to run the gamut, and no one seems to be taking notes for commitment to a nursing home any more.

While I treasure my children and have always enjoyed being honored each year on Mother's Day, I've never believed parents should live specifically for the birth of their progeny's offspring, and I never asked my older son, Beau, and his wife, Leila, when that might happen, though I was delighted to learn they were "in the family way" about three years back.

The birth of Margaret McLaurin Beasley in 2001 turned all our lives upside down. She's a siren who now answers to Maggie, Maggie McB and The Magster, but she also comes running with arms open wide when I beckon her with Magamuffin and Magpie or, when she is especially sweet, NiNi's Angel Baby.

Children's angelic faces make it impossible not to be captivated by their innocence. While that's easily understood, something really strange happens to normal reasoning upon becoming a grandparent. My wallet, once held firmly in check, suddenly seems accordion-like, pliable and ready to fall wide open at a moment's notice for pint-sized acquisitions. Almost overnight, my house filled with a multitude of miniature books, music boxes and sippy cups. Sometimes I find myself strolling through the children's section in stores, looking at lacy dresses and shiny red patent-leather shoes, quite a change from the cowboy boots and GI Joe outfits my two boys enjoyed wearing.

Grandparenting is such a universal experience, a certain kind of kinship. I often compare notes with Robert Johnston, who was in my 1963 graduating class at Manchester High. Robert and his wife, Sally, have one son and one daughter. While Robert, who grew up with three brothers, always has a pleasant look on his face, speaking of his four granddaughters adds an extra lilt to his ever-present grin.

Another good friend and neighbor, Betty Jo (BJ) Bridgforth, and I often share stories and photos of our grandchildren. Since BJ gives computers a wide berth, it seemed natural that I'd be the go-between when her son Jody and his family were stationed in Germany for two tours of Army duty. Jody, a helicopter pilot during both American invasions in Iraq; his wife, Sunisa; and their three children were re-assigned recently to Fort Rucker in Alabama. Christmas came early for the Bridgforth family in 2004. Alexander Shea, Jody and Sunisa's second son and fourth child, made his debut on Dec. 23. On Christmas Eve, I had the privilege of showing BJ a digital photo of her precious new grandson. BJ and I frequently discuss the difference between children and grandchildren, the antics of the latter being a ready source of laughter.

It made my day recently when Leila, my daughter-in-law, called and asked me to "cheer up" Maggie. It seems the little darling got too close to Dickens, the resident cat. Dickens is usually patient, but there is a limit, which Maggie learned when she was scratched that day. Still whimpering, Maggie listened as I consoled her by explaining that Dickens evidently had had a bad day and needed to rest. I could almost see her sucking her thumb and bobbing her little head up and down in agreement. Within minutes, she was laughing and jabbering, as if I had made the world right again.

I've always believed that being a mother was a sacred trust. I learned so much from my mother and never miss her more than when Mother's Day approaches. This year, I've thought a lot about her mother, Salina Katheryn "Cass" Sutphin, whom all the grandchildren lovingly called Big Granny. One of my most special childhood memories is of the times when I took up my station behind my grandmother as she sat in a living room chair. She would take the pins from the "bun" on top of her head and let her silken white hair tumble down over the back of the wooden chair rungs, reaching almost to the floor. It always amazed me that it was seldom tangled. I'd gently brush her hair, which had never been cut, as Big Granny praised my dexterity.

When our first son was born, my husband, Oscar, and I made a beeline for Radford, Va., to show him off to Big Granny. Four years later, she was quite ill when our second son was born. Jason was barely 6 weeks old when we headed toward Radford again. Nothing in the world can compare to how I felt when I placed my babies in their great-grandmother's arms. Somehow, it was like she was imparting a blessing on their lives, as she had done for me. Big Granny said something one time that has always stuck with me: "When children are little, they step on your toes; when they're big, they step on your heart."

Mothers and grandmothers alike help shoulder their children's cares, no matter the child's age. For months, I've been comforting Lois Davis, a dear friend who lives in Falmouth with her husband, Bill. All three of Lois' sons have been in Iraq in the area near Baghdad, known as the "Sunni Triangle." Matt, the oldest, formerly trained in military special operations with the Army, was part of an elite private security team contracted to provide protection for American civilians. Twins Adam and Jason served in military operations in Tikrit, Saddam Hussein's hometown, and in Mosul, respectively. Adam, career Army, is stationed in Germany with his family, and Jason, who lives with his family in Richmond, was called to active duty with the Army Reserve.

Extra encouragement was necessary when Jason was wounded. Traveling in the last truck of a convoy, his vehicle was hit by a rocket-propelled grenade, leaving him with numerous cuts and hearing impairment. Meanwhile Matt's body armor repelled a bullet during an attack in which his rear gunner was killed. My computer fairly crackled on Feb. 22 with the joyous news that Jason had made a full recovery (albeit with lingering hearing loss) and that all three of Lois' boys had returned home to their families.

It seems Mother's Day can come early, too. ≋

May 2005

58

No Escape from Red Tape
Getting caught in a never-ending bureaucratic nightmare

T HERE IS SOMETHING VERY disconcerting about having a police officer knock on your door, especially when he's holding a piece of paper in his hand.

This has happened to me on two occasions since I've been living in Chesterfield County. Each time, it terrified me because, as a freelance writer, I can turn in work months ahead of time, but I'm not paid until it publishes, which means I live way too close to the edge. Seeing those officers approaching, with warrants in hand, made me wonder if I had robbed Peter to pay Paul one too many times. But I digress.

The warrants were both addressed to a young man whose last name is the same as mine. Each time, I carefully explained to the deputy that I had lived in my present address for almost 10 years, and that the individual, if he had ever lived in my house at all, had not done so in the last decade. I also pointed out that when I bought the house, it had been owned for years by the same person, but his name wasn't Beasley.

I thought it was especially odd when, about two years ago, I received a letter from a high school principal, directing me to call the principal's office to discuss my "son's" inappropriate name-calling and his suspension from school.

I should interject at this point that: 1) neither of my sons ever attended school in this area; 2) they both lived in northern Virginia at the time; and 3) they were each over 30 and college graduates. But I digress again.

I called the principal and left messages for three days. I wanted to personally advise him that the allocated time frame for the child's caregivers to contact him was quickly running out.

When I finally did reach him, he was astonished to learn that: 1) this individual did not live at my address, nor was I responsible for him; and 2) extremely personal information, emanating from his office, had been revealed about an underage student. I assured him I would destroy the letter if he promised to find the appropriate caregivers and change the address on the school file.

After muttering something about it being his secretary's fault, which I found very annoying, he apologized and said the matter would be rectified. Are you surprised I didn't receive a letter thanking me for correcting the situation? Neither was I, but I digress yet again.

Fast forward to March 30, 2005. It was a beautiful sun-shiny day, during which I left the door open to invite fresh air inside as I worked in my office toward the back of the house. In the late afternoon, I decided to stretch my legs, stood up from typing and went to retrieve the mail. Returning to my house, I found a paper affixed to my storm door with a rubber band. I must not have heard the doorbell.

There it was—a third service for the same individual, subpoenaing him to appear as a witness for a criminal case. It listed the man with my address and, this time, my phone number. It distressed me, but I decided to be like Scarlett O'Hara in *Gone With the Wind* and save it for another day.

The next morning I called the number on the subpoena, the Chesterfield Circuit Court, Criminal Division.

Karla Viar, a deputy clerk and supervisor of that office, answered the phone. She carefully explained that the clerk's office receives information and addresses from attorneys and processes subpoenas based on that information. I gave her the case number on the subpoena, and she searched for the file. She came back to the phone, saying she couldn't locate the file immediately. Not wanting to keep me waiting, she suggested I call the attorney whose name was listed on the subpoena.

I placed the call. The attorney listened while, like a broken record, I explained the situation again.

He said, "The court sends out those papers," to which I replied, "A clerk just advised me that subpoenas are sent to addresses supplied by attorneys."

"What's your address?" he asked. I could hear him ruffling through his files. Several minutes lapsed. He asked, "What's your name?" More ruffling. And then the ringer, "Well, don't you know him?"

I wanted to ask, "Do you know everybody in Richmond with your last name?" Instead I asked if he was the aforementioned man's counsel, to which he fairly shouted, "I don't have to answer any of your questions."

Shocked at his tone of voice, I queried, "Let me get this straight: I'm holding a subpoena with your name and phone number on it as a contact person. The subpoena has been sent from a criminal court to someone I don't know, but it has my personal address and phone number on it, and you don't want to help me resolve it?"

He raised his voice even more, hollered, "Lady, I got to get off this phone!" and slammed down the receiver.

Stunned speechless, it made me wonder what was next. Would I wake one night to find a SWAT team knocking down my door with a search warrant, of course, to the wrong address?

I sat wondering what to do for a long time. The silence was finally broken by my phone ringing. Although it was almost 6:30 p.m., it was Judy Worthington, Circuit Court Clerk for Chesterfield County. She said she was sorry I had a problem and offered to help.

For the second time that day, I was speechless. Her gracious manner almost made up for the aforementioned jerk's behavior. She explained she would put a note in the case in question.

I later learned that another subpoena had been posted on the door where the man actually lived on

April 7, so that was some consolation, but it turned out to be a moot point. The case, scheduled for April 13, was nol prossed, or not prosecuted.

Still wondering what I might do to avoid the situation in the future, I called Ms. Worthington again on April 21. Although sympathetic, she explained it was a Catch-22, saying, "There is no link to tie cases together to prevent a subsequent problem if the same witness were being subpoenaed in multiple cases unrelated to the current one. While this particular case may be resolved, there is nothing in place to keep it from happening again."

There is something wrong when an innocent individual does everything humanly possible to rectify a problem they didn't create, and yet, it still exists. It's like fighting with an insurance company or a kangaroo, an exercise in futility most of the time.

I threw up my hands in defeat and turned my attention to booking an airplane ticket for an upcoming trip to Poland. I held on forever listening to messages and instructions, pressed just about every number on my phone's keypad and finally got a recording—in Spanish. ≋

June 2005

59

Meditations on the Birth of a Nation
Trip to Virginia's Historic Triangle elicits feeling of patriotism

THERE I WAS, ON THE verge of tears, standing with a group of media representatives near the banks of the James River. No. No one was insulting me. In fact, I was very comfortable as part of a gaggle of writers brought together for a media tour of numerous goings-on planned for the upcoming celebration of the 400th anniversary of the Jamestown landing.

At first, I was busy taking notes. Then I happened to catch the sun's rays bouncing off the shimmering water and noticed that it seemed to be endless. Unconsciously, I stopped writing and got lost in thinking of the hardships that the first women must have endured on the trip from England and particularly after they arrived. I, who have given birth twice in a modern hospital, tried to imagine facing pregnancy and the ordeal of bringing a child into the world with little or no medical assistance, not to speak of the absence of running water and electricity.

I suddenly thought of my daughter-in-law and what a difficult time she recently had breast-feeding both of my grandchildren. It necessitated visits from a lactation specialist to get things going. I wondered how many women had grieved over the deaths of babies in the New World, deaths brought on simply for lack of sustenance or archaic living conditions.

Thinking about that reminded me one of the stories my mother used to tell about my father. It seems that after my brother and oldest sister were born in my parents' tiny home in the foothills of the Blue Ridge Mountains of Virginia, the general practitioner who delivered them became exasperated. He offered to knock $10 off the delivery bill for my middle sister and for me if my father agreed to transport my mother to the hospital, where he could actually see what he was doing.

No amount of cash on hand could have affected the outcome for those brave souls who stepped onto land for the first time at Jamestown.

The water surrounding the landing was supposed to have swallowed up the original fort site long ago, at least that's what has been told to groups of schoolchildren for what seems like eons. Now, thanks to the discovery of the perimeter walls of the actual fort site, historical updates are ongoing.

I stood by the river within yards of where some of the many volunteers were digging away and sifting dirt. During the tour, I was privy to the "inside" story of all the newest discoveries and had the wonderful opportunity of seeing priceless artifacts, including the skeleton of a man with a bullet lodged in the bend of his knee. The curating staff jokingly refers to the remains as "J.R." It took me a minute to connect the dots between the skeleton and the *Dallas* television show.

Modernity isn't what the many teams working on Virginia's Historic Triangle are aiming for. Representatives from Williamsburg, Yorktown and Jamestown are aiming for authenticity, providing a taste of what life was like for our forebears so many years ago. The National Park Service, a major contributor in preparing for the 2007 celebrations, actually started its work several years ago, not knowing then what an important part they were playing.

Between 1931 and 1934, the park service restored the Moore House, the site in Yorktown where surrender negotiations for the end of the Revolutionary War were worked out. As I stood inside the tiny wooden house, now painted white with green shutters, I wondered how the uniformed British Army officers felt knowing they were surrendering to a ragtag group of revolutionaries, many of them just teenagers.

Later I stood where a British Army officer surrendered a sword in defeat, severing our constitutional ties with England forever. It seems that Lord Cornwallis, perhaps not feeling well, refused to attend the ceremony. When Washington would not accept the sword from a lesser-ranking officer, the man had to offer the sword two additional times before actually finding an officer who would accept it. Our park guide described how one of the British soldiers wept as he joined his fellow soldiers in laying down his musket, the final act of a defeated army.

Remnants of the war are part and parcel as part of the history of Colonial Williamsburg, along with the many restored sites of that time. One of the fascinating remnants of that era is hearing the tune of an approaching fife and drum corps while watching the large horses pull wagons of visitors through town, providing a bird's-eye view of the many historical sites.

As a former farm girl, another treat for me was visiting the livery and seeing the rare breeds of livestock of that era, including the fighting gamecocks (now retired), still living in the midst of the settlement as they must have done centuries ago.

The lingering effect and contributions of the Powhatan Indians and African slaves to the new world are unmistakable and too numerous to write about in such a small space. I simply couldn't take it all in. I finally gave up on that and decided that a return trip was a must.

What struck me during the two-day event was just how little I really know about the details of this historical period and what an awesome feeling it was to stand on the brink of the United States and walk the same path trod by those early brave souls. It's amazing to me that we have become such staunch allies with a country we once struggled against for our freedom. I don't know about other Americans, but I've always wanted to visit England and see where it all started, on the other side of that seemingly limitless James River.

Tears are welling up in my eyes again just thinking of my experience. It's the same feeling I get whenever a U.S. flag passes me in a military formation or I hear the national anthem sung. I can't imagine the laborious early efforts made for a new country where all Americans, and now so many immigrants, enjoy the fruits of untold and undocumented sacrifice. It reminds me of one of my favorite sayings, which goes something like this: The only reason a person can see into the future is because he is standing on the shoulders of others.

Happy Fourth of July. ≋

July 2005

60

Color's Cure
Virginia's poet laureate offers much-needed inspiration

I KEPT THINKING OF black and white as Rita Dove, who is black, captivated an audience of at least 100 students and older adults, mostly white, including her husband, at the Midlothian Campus of John Tyler Community College.

Dove was the keynote speaker at the 10th Annual Women's Literary Program. A first-timer, I attended because I desperately needed a break from work. My morning started slow, the same way every morning had since the completion of my first book, *Izzy's Fire,* a few months earlier.

I was exhausted from spending the previous seven years researching the dark events of the Holocaust. Now, between signings and marketing the book, I was also frantically developing free-lance pieces for financial survival. Yet,once again, I was thinking of beginning a book.

"Are you crazy?" I asked myself.

"Definitely," I answered.

I just had to find a way to see brightness again through another literary venue. Besides that, people kept asking a recurring question: "What's your next book about?" I decided to collect some of the columns I've been writing for *Richmond Magazine* since 1998 into a book and go for broke.

I was discussing that possibility with Sally Huband, a dear friend, when I jokingly said I'd title it *Reflections of a Purple Zebra*. It made sense to me immediately. My column is named "Reflections," and I've always loved zebras and admired the fact that their stripes, like human fingerprints, are individual and never duplicated. I'm convinced that had I been born a zebra, my stripes would have been purple, my favorite color.

Attempting a second book was a "fur piece" to jump, as my late father would have said in his country way. However, I thrive on challenges and believed the hurdles weren't that high. Wrong answer. No matter how much I tried, the intense fire I needed to keep the book project alive kept fizzling out.

Suddenly all my work became drudgery. While I've griped about long hours and low pay before, I've doggedly kept writing, believing that personal satisfaction oftentimes balanced the monetary sacrifices I've had to make.

Working alone has a great benefit. I only work with one—how can I say this—one rear end, the one looking back at me in the bathroom mirror every morning. The professional world being full of, uh, rear ends, this had always motivated me to remain my own boss. However, years of balancing freelance jobs barely left me enough strength to walk this spring.

And then along came Rita Dove, former U.S. poet laureate, current poet laureate of Virginia and Commonwealth English professor at the University of Virginia, with eyes flashing and fingernails brightly painted, wearing a sexy, three-ruffled beige skirt and a black, white and beige sleeveless top with a scoop neck that showed off her gold and onyx necklace and the quarter-sized gold medallions dancing from her ears.

Her blouse was pulled over the skirt, which bunched out in the back, like she might have been wearing a slip, but I wasn't sure. She didn't seem the slightest bit worried about that or that her tummy pooched out in front as she swayed and rocked, using her hands to punctuate the word scenes she was painting with her voice.

I unconsciously lifted my pen and began capturing the moment. I jotted notes about the deep scar off center at her left temple, the little gap between her otherwise even white teeth, her luminous brown eyes, ringed with smoky color and mascara, her hair in tiny rivulets—so perfect I couldn't decide whether it was natural or a wig, and even the smallpox vaccination on her left arm, like the matching one I had gotten as a child. She seemed electric, emanating pulses of energy that fell on me like rain on a parched desert.

What touched me deeply, though, was the way Dove described her own struggles. She told of shallow times when she felt empty, much like the funk I was currently experiencing. She spoke of leaving poems untouched for months on end and later going back to breathe life into them. She paced as she talked, taking in the whole roomful of people with her wide-eyed gaze, understanding that we, the writer enfants, needed the lesson she was imparting. She said that, in the end, the reward of getting our words down on paper was worth what had to be endured.

It struck me that, besides being inspired, I was actually experiencing history. More than 40 years ago, my father was determined that I, the last of his four children, wouldn't go to school with any blacks, and God help any interracial couple in Richmond, Va., during the 1960s.

I laughed inwardly with joy. What a leap, to go from graduating from an all-white high school to coming full circle in the same county and having the opportunity of seeing — not to speak of admiring — a black woman who had come a "fur piece" by anybody's measuring stick.

Dove mesmerized me with her expressive hands. I couldn't resist asking why she painted blue, red, green, gold and purple diagonal stripes on her fingernails, leaving half of each nail its natural buff color. With a laugh, she explained it was a carryover from her teen years, and because she "loved color" so much, she just kept doing it. She also explained that it took years to finally decide she wasn't crazy for adhering to her inner voice or for working on several projects simultaneously. She even said she keeps her literary works in different colored folders, a practice I also follow.

It suddenly became clearer to me why I had to write about purple zebras. In fact, I was wearing a purple sweater, which Dove referred to, when she explained the "need" to have color in her life.

Naturally I bought one of Dove's books, *Mother Love*. She picked up her pen, thought for a moment and then wrote, "For Nancy, who likes color as much as I do."

I hugged Dove afterward and told her I believed I would write about her one day. I didn't know then that she would eventually become the subject of this column and thus, part of my next book, but I did know she wasn't black *or* white.

Maybe a rainbow. ≋

November 2005

Meditation

People are often unreliable, illogical and self-centered;
forgive them anyway.
If you are kind, people may accuse you of selfish,
ulterior motives; be kind anyway.
If you are successful, you will win some false friends
and true enemies; succeed anyway.
If you are honest and frank, people may cheat you; be
honest and frank anyway.
What you spend your years building, someone may
destroy overnight; build it anyway.
The good you do today, people will often forget tomor-
row; do good anyway.
Give the world the best you have and it may never be
enough; give the world the best you've got anyway.
You see, in the final analysis, it is between
you and God.
It never was between you and them anyway.

— Mother Theresa

About the Author

Nancy Wright Beasley started her journalism journey in 1979 as a state correspondent for *The Richmond News Leader*. She resigned in 1986 and *(worked in)* advertising and layout for a variety of publications in the Southside Virginia area. Following several more years in economic development and public relations work, she ultimately settled in Richmond, Va., in 1994, launching a freelance writing career and becoming a columnist and contributing editor for *Richmond Magazine* in 1998.

In 2000, Beasley earned a master's degree at the School of Mass Communications at Virginia Commonwealth University where she now teaches. The Virginia Press Women named her as their Communicator of Achievement in 2005. The Richmond YWCA chose her as one of 10 Outstanding Women in Central Virginia in 2006.

Beasley's first nonfiction book, *Izzy's Fire: Finding Humanity in the Holocaust,* was nominated for a People's Choice Award, a competition sponsored by the James River Writers and the Library of Virginia. The book is now being taught in numerous schools and universities in several states.

The author lives in Richmond and is currently pursuing a master of fine arts degree in children's literature at Hollins University.